Cambridge Ele

Elements in Public Economics
edited by
Robin Boadway
Queen's University
Frank A. Cowell
The London School of Economics and Political Science
Massimo Florio
University of Milan

MIXED OLIGOPOLY AND PUBLIC ENTERPRISES

Joanna Poyago-Theotoky
University of Salento,
University of East Anglia and
The Australian National University

CAMBRIDGE
UNIVERSITY PRESS

CAMBRIDGE
UNIVERSITY PRESS

Shaftesbury Road, Cambridge CB2 8EA, United Kingdom

One Liberty Plaza, 20th Floor, New York, NY 10006, USA

477 Williamstown Road, Port Melbourne, VIC 3207, Australia

314–321, 3rd Floor, Plot 3, Splendor Forum, Jasola District Centre, New Delhi – 110025, India

103 Penang Road, #05–06/07, Visioncrest Commercial, Singapore 238467

Cambridge University Press is part of Cambridge University Press & Assessment, a department of the University of Cambridge.

We share the University's mission to contribute to society through the pursuit of education, learning and research at the highest international levels of excellence.

www.cambridge.org
Information on this title: www.cambridge.org/9781009486750

DOI: 10.1017/9781108770279

First published 2024

A catalogue record for this publication is available from the British Library.

ISBN 978-1-009-48675-0 Hardback
ISBN 978-1-108-72624-5 Paperback
ISSN 2516-2276 (online)
ISSN 2516-2268 (print)

Mixed Oligopoly and Public Enterprises

Elements in Public Economics

DOI: 10.1017/9781108770279
First published online: April 2024

Joanna Poyago-Theotoky
University of Salento,
University of East Anglia and
The Australian National University

Author for correspondence: Joanna Poyago-Theotoky,
joanna.poyago-theotoky@unisalento.it

Abstract: This Element offers a review and synthesis of the theoretical analysis of mixed oligopoly, that is a hybrid market structure in which public (state-owned) and private firms interact, using a variety of strategic variables. A distinguishing feature of a mixed oligopoly is that firms have different objectives. A public firm's objective is a notion of social welfare while a private firm is profit-maximising. Privatisation and partial privatisation of a public firm is also discussed, together with several applications from diverse subfields spanning industrial organisation, applied microeconomic theory, innovation, international trade, and environment policy. The author also discusses ways in which the original analysis has been enriched to study the interaction between providers of public sector services as opposed to traditional goods.

Keywords: public enterprise, state-owned enterprise, public firm, mixed oligopoly, privatisation

JEL classifications: L32, H42, H44, D43

ISBNs: 9781009486750 (HB), 9781108726245 (PB), 9781108770279 (OC)
ISSNs: 2516-2276 (online), 2516-2268 (print)

Contents

1 Introduction

A mixed oligopoly is defined as an oligopolistic market structure where a good (or service) is provided by a relatively small number of firms possessing market power and the objective of at least one of them (usually a public enterprise[1]) differs from that of the other competing firms (De Fraja & Delbono, 1990, p. 1). Since the authoritative survey of De Fraja and Delbono (1990) there has been a flurry of research on the topic of mixed oligopoly, considered now a mature research field spanning contributions from industrial organisation, applied microeconomic theory, public economics and beyond, but no detailed survey to review these recent developments. It is therefore essential to provide an account of what we have learned as well as to discuss current issues that need to be explored further. This is our aim in this present Element.

The rationale for having a public firm operate alongside private profit-maximising firms is based on the perception that a public firm, by way of its *objective to improve social welfare, can act as a regulatory instrument* and as such correct, or alleviate at least, market failures associated with imperfect or distorted competition. Exploring whether indeed a public firm can be effective in this has been a common theme in the theoretical literature on mixed oligopoly. Associated issues relate to privatisation or partial-privatisation of public firms or the opposite, that is, nationalisation or creation of new public firms, the optimal extent of government participation in these and so on.

Over the last few decades, there have been arguments in favour of, or against, the privatisation of state-owned enterprises. Many Western countries have privatised large public or state-owned enterprises in many sectors once considered strategic. More recently, though, following the global financial crisis of 2008 (GFC) and the COVID-19 pandemic, there is a reversal in the privatisation activity and intensity of previous times, with governments often creating new state-owned firms who then operate alongside competing private firms. We therefore provide a simple, yet thorough, explanation of the main theoretical framework used to analyse the interaction between public and private firms, paying particular attention to the formulation of the objective function of a public firm (total surplus or a weighted combination of its components, usually consumer surplus and firms' profits), technology and cost structure, and order of moves. Then we review a distinctive and select number of applications and extensions of this basic framework, in essence providing the reader

---

[1] In what follows we use the term 'public' firm to refer to a public enterprise, or an enterprise that is state-owned, in line with the majority of the literature on mixed oligopoly that this Element surveys.

with a signposted path to a swath of material that has been published on the topic, while conveying our view of the larger field.

We then discuss in more detail what we believe are three important areas where the framework of mixed oligopoly has most recently been applied, as an ideal analytical tool, and where additional research is needed. In particular, we consider the following:

1. Quality provision by public providers (e.g., health services, education, transport, postal services)
2. Environmental policy and corporate social responsibility
3. Extrinsic rewards versus intrinsic motivation and their effect on the management of a public enterprise.

The selection of these three areas is guided by the following considerations: (1) quality is by far a major characteristic in the provision of several services where public and private providers co-exist, (2) environmental issues are a manifestation of extensive negative externalities so that considering the presence of even a single public firm internalising these externalities may have beneficial effects, and (3) accounting for intrinsic motivation can shift the focus from ownership of a public firm and the objectives of principals towards selection and motivation of managers, which in turn can be important in mixed markets such as, for example, healthcare provision. Of course, this selection does not mean that price and quantity issues are not important, on the contrary. Rather, it serves to highlight a historical perspective in that the extant mixed oligopoly literature has been exploring quantity and price effects since its inception, whereas the selected areas represent much more recent research.

We begin in Section 2 by presenting some basic information on the definition and presence of public firms and mixed oligopoly. We then present in detail the classical or canonical model of mixed oligopoly, starting from basic principles. Next, in Section 3, we discuss the concept of partial privatisation and the associated alternative objective of a public firm. In Section 4 we present a selection of applications stemming from the previous two sections, drawing from diverse areas such as industrial organisation, international trade, R&D and innovation, as well as a discussion of the privatisation neutrality theorem. In Section 5 we consider some pertinent current issues where the focus is shifted on providers of public services (health, education) and the importance of quality, environmental aspects, banking and finance, and finally the role of intrinsic motivation in public firms. Finally we draw some concluding remarks in Section 6.

2 Traditional Mixed Oligopoly

As the main focus of this Element is the public firm (or enterprise) and its interaction with private firms in the market, we need to describe the notion of a public enterprise. In the simplest terms, a public enterprise is an economic entity where the state has significant ownership or control. An alternative and widely used term is state-owned enterprise (SOE). The definition of a SOE according to OECD (2017) is quite broad:

> A state-owned enterprise is any corporate entity recognised by national law as an enterprise and in which the central level of government exercises ownership and control. This includes joint stock companies, limited liability companies and partnerships limited by shares. In addition, statutory corporations, whose legal personality is established through specific legislation, should be considered as SOEs if they engage in economic activities, either exclusively or together with the pursuit of public policy objectives. An economic activity is one that involves offering goods or services on a given market and which could, at least in principle, be carried out by a private operator in order to make profits. Quasi-corporations, which are autonomous commercial activities carried out inside the general government sector, should be considered as SOEs if they are financially autonomous and charge economically significant prices.

The European Union (EU) uses a slightly different definition provided in the European System of Accounts (ESA2010),[2] which basically translates to:

> SOEs can therefore include in particular the following categories:
> - companies fully owned by public authorities;
> - companies where public authorities have a majority share;
> - companies where public authorities retain a minority share but have special statutory powers;
> - companies where public authorities have a minority share and no special powers. These are generally not considered as SOEs however they may be of relevance in order to obtain a fuller picture of governments' stake in the economy (European Commission, 2016, p. 6–7).

We shall use the term 'public firm' to refer to a firm that is state-owned (fully or partially) and to encompass the above definitions. For the purposes of this Element, and in line with the extensive literature on mixed oligopoly, the main distinguishing feature between a public and a private firm lies in their different

---

[2] Eurostat (2013) states: The public non-financial corporations subsector consists of all non-financial corporations, quasi-corporations and non-profit institutions, recognised as independent legal entities, that are market producers and are subject to control by government units (ESA2010, 2.51, p. 35).

objectives, so our working definition of a public firm is an entity whose object-ive is to maximise a notion of social welfare, whereas a private firm aims to maximise profit.

Public firms have a long history dating back to ancient Egypt (Rostovtzeff (1926, p. 607) and Warburton (1997)). More recently, and following the 'privat-isation era' of the 1980s, public firms are becoming important again, especially following the 2008 global financial crisis (GFC) and the 2019 COVID pan-demic. State-owned firms are mostly prevalent in strategic sectors of an economy such as energy, minerals, infrastructure, telecommunications, broad-casting, other utilities, and, in some countries, financial services and transport.[3] A recent report by the OECD (OECD, 2017) provides detailed information on the presence of SOEs based on a dataset covering forty countries and including China where SOEs are prevalent.[4] Despite its shortcomings relating to extent of coverage and type of SOEs, this report establishes the fact that SOEs are important actors in many economies.

The standard economic reasoning for the existence of public firms views them as a solution to correct market failures, especially in the case of nat-ural monopolies (utilities, water, etc.), especially in the absence of other forms of regulation,[5] or when competition is not viable.[6] The main characteristics of natural monopoly are: (i) the presence of increasing returns in production (decreasing average cost) and (ii) the level of demand is insufficient to support more than a single profitable firm.[7] Figure 1 illustrates an elementary case, where the production technology is characterised by large fixed/sunk costs and a constant marginal cost (MC) giving rise to a decreasing average cost (AC). The efficient outcome associated with perfect competition, q_c, is given where marginal cost equals price ($MC = AR_1$), with AR_1 representing total demand, D_1. Obviously, this outcome is unobtainable. When there is a monopoly in this market, the profit-maximising output is q_1^m with associated price p^m, which covers the associated average cost, AC, hence the monopolist is profitable. Should a second firm operate in this market, so that the two firms share it

---

[3] See Bognetti (2020) for a historical account of state enterprises in Western economies and Bird (2020) for a more general overview.

[4] For additional information see the live document on www.oecd.org/daf/ca/soemarket.htm.

[5] Recall that the market failure could be corrected by price regulation so that price is set at marginal cost and the resulting loss covered by a subsidy in which case the correction of the natural monopoly does not necessitate a public firm.

[6] An alternative solution is regulation, a vast topic of research and practice but outside the scope of this Element.

[7] See the classical textbooks on public economics by Hindriks and Myles (2013) and Stiglitz and Rosengard (2015).

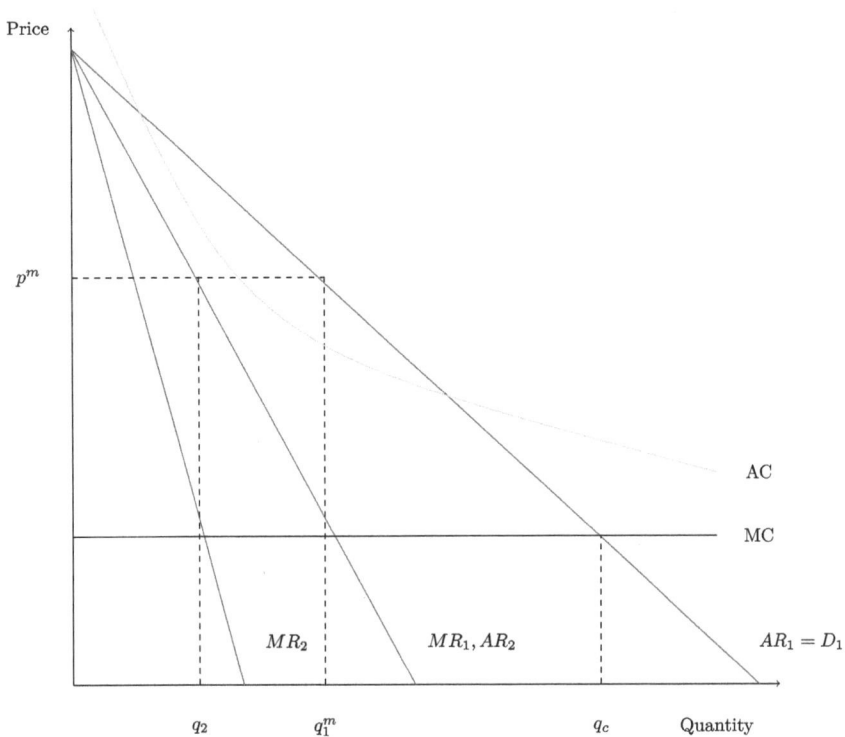

Figure 1 Natural monopoly.

equally,[8] the demand facing each one of them becomes AR_2, and they each produce q_2 but the profit-maximising price p^m is below average cost, leading to a loss for both firms.

Leaving aside the case of natural monopolies, public firms have been operating in a number of oligopolistic industries, in what is referred as *mixed oligopoly*, that is, a concentrated and imperfectly competitive market where interacting firms have different objectives (De Fraja & Delbono, 1990). A public firm, as a state-owned enterprise, can be a policy tool used by governments to correct market failures and improve resource allocation in imperfectly competitive markets, an argument that has been initially put forward by Merrill and Schneider (1966) in their seminal contribution that has inaugurated this research field: A public firm operates in a mixed oligopoly, an intermediate market structure between the extremes of 'complete government ownership

---

[8] Note that it is not always the case that firms will share the market equally. There are instances where an entrant would just get what is left by the incumbent; for example, see Ceriani and Florio (2011).

and control, and private ownership restricted by close government supervision in the form of regulation and anti-trust laws' (Merrill & Schneider, 1966, p. 400).

The starting point is to provide a simple, yet thorough, understanding of the basic framework used in the theoretical analysis of mixed oligopoly. The defining characteristic in a mixed oligopoly is the co-existence in the market of one or more public firms, competing with private firms that have market power. Traditionally, the objective of the public firm is to maximise social welfare, while the private firms are profit-maximisers.

Consider an oligopolistic market for a homogeneous good provided by n private profit-maximising firms indexed by $i \in \{1, \ldots, n\}$ and m public firms, indexed by $j \in \{n + 1, \ldots, n + m\}$, maximising a notion of social welfare, most often total surplus. Suppose the inverse market demand is given by

$$p = p(Q) = p(q_1 + \ldots + q_n, q_{n+1}, \ldots, q_{n+m}) = p\left(\sum_{i=1}^{n} q_i + \sum_{j=n+1}^{m} q_j\right) \quad (1)$$

where p is price and Q stands for aggregate output, with $p'(Q) < 0$ and $p''(Q) \le 0$, and q_i, q_j, denoting the quantities produced by individual firms, private and public, respectively. On the cost side, suppose that all firms face the same cost conditions, with total cost per firm given by

$$c_r = c(q_r), r = i, j, i \ne j \quad (2)$$

with c_r twice continuously differentiable, $c'(q_r) \ge 0$ and $c''(q_r) \ge 0$. The payoff for a private firm i is given by its profit

$$\pi_i(q) = p(Q)q_i - c_i(q_i) = p\left(\sum_{i=1}^{n} q_i + \sum_{j=n+1}^{m} q_j\right)q_i - c_i(q_i) \quad (3)$$

where $q = (q_1, \ldots, q_{n+m})$. For a public firm j, the payoff function is captured by social welfare, or total surplus, given by

$$W_j(q) = \int_{t=0}^{Q} p(t)dt - \sum_{r=1}^{n+m} c(q_r). \quad (4)$$

An alternative, widely used, but equivalent, objective consists of the sum of all firms profits and consumer surplus (De Fraja & Delbono, 1990, pp. 7–8)

$$W_j(q) = \sum_{r=1}^{n+m} \pi_r(q) + \int_{t=0}^{Q} (p(t) - p(Q))dt.$$

We now proceed to characterise the Nash equilibrium in this market, where private and public firms compete by setting output: q^* is a Nash equilibrium if the following conditions hold:

1. for all $i \in \{1, \ldots, n\}$, $\pi_i(q^*) \geq \pi_i(q^*|q_i)$, for all q_i
2. for all $j \in \{n+1, \ldots, n+m\}$, $W_j(q^*) \geq W_j(q^*|q_j)$, for all q_j.

To begin with, we consider a special case where the cost function, (2), is linear

$$c_r = cq_r, r = i, j, i \neq j, c > 0. \tag{5}$$

This technology represents constant returns to scale with a constant marginal cost (c), the same for all firms and there are no fixed costs. It turns out that the Nash equilibrium has all private firms producing zero output and only the public firms sharing production of the good, with total output being equal to the perfectly competitive outcome, and price being equal to marginal cost.[9] To understand why this is indeed the case, suppose that q^* is the equilibrium output and $p(Q^*) = c$. If not, then a public firm could improve its position by changing its output. Then, for every private firm i, $\pi_i(q^*) = p(Q^*)q_i^* - cq_i^* = 0$. If $q_i^* > 0$, by reducing production firm i can raise price and earn positive profit, a contradiction. Thus, q_i^* must be zero. Adding a small fixed cost yields the result where only one public firm is producing the competitive equilibrium output and all other firms cease operation. These (rather unsatisfactory) equilibrium outcomes, public oligopoly or public monopoly yielding the efficient allocation, are the direct consequence of assuming linear production costs, the same for all firms.

To make further progress and obtain more intuitive and/or general results, we have to either consider convex costs (with rising marginal costs, i.e., decreasing returns to scale) or allow for constant, but differing, marginal costs between public and private firms. For now we shall concentrate on the first solution, introduced by De Fraja and Delbono (1989) in their seminal contribution, as this has become what we call the *canonical* model in the theory of mixed oligopoly.[10]

Suppose that there is a single public firm, $m = 1$, so that we can simplify and consider the $n + 1$ oligopoly, and index firms by i: the set of all firms is $I = \{0, 1, 2, \ldots, n\}$ with $i = 0$ indicating the public firm. De Fraja and Delbono (1989) specify the cost function (2) in the following manner:

$$c_i(q_i) = f + \frac{k}{2}q_i^2, f, k > 0, \tag{6}$$

---

[9] This unsatisfactory outcome is referred to as 'Cournot paradox' by Nett (1993).
[10] For earlier surveys on mixed oligopoly see De Fraja and Delbono (1990) and Bös (1994).

that is, they introduce increasing marginal costs ($k > 0$) and fixed costs ($f > 0$). On the demand side, the inverse demand function is linear and, in particular (1), becomes

$$p = a - Q, \ a > 0, \tag{7}$$

where a represents the size of the market.

We can now address questions pertaining to the desirability of a public firm operating in a market with other private firms and the associated issue of privatisation. As De Fraja and Delbono (1989) show, in the mixed oligopoly equilibrium (designated by the superscript M), the public firm's output is

$$q_0^M = \frac{a(k + 1)}{(1 + k^2) + nk}$$

and each private firm, $i = 1, \ldots, n$, produces

$$q_i^M = \frac{ak}{(1 + k^2) + nk},$$

and it is obvious that $q_0^M > q_i^M$, the public firm produces a larger amount than each private firm independently. It is also easy to see that the public firm sets output at a price equal to marginal cost. Social welfare is given by

$$W^M = \frac{a^2[(1 + k)^3 + nk(nk + 2 + 4k + k^2)]}{2[(1 + k^2) + nk]^2} - (n + 1)f.$$

In the case of the fully private oligopoly (indexed by the superscript P), all $n+1$ firms maximise profit; this corresponds to having the public firm privatised and allows a simple comparison between the mixed economy (before privatisation) and the private economy (after privatisation). Each firm produces

$$q_i^P = \frac{a}{2 + k + n}$$

and social welfare is

$$W^P = \frac{a^2[(3 + k) + (4 + k)n + n^2]}{2(2 + k + n)^2} - (n + 1)f.$$

Hence privatisation of the public firm shall improve welfare only if $W^P > W^M$. In a major result, De Fraja and Delbono (1989) establish that this is indeed true when the number of private firms is relatively large (hence privatisation is desirable); otherwise, it is best to retain the public firm in public hands.[11]

---

[11] The desirability or not of privatisation continues to be a lively research topic; for example, see the recent contributions by Haraguchi, Matsumura, and Yoshida (2018), Haraguchi and Matsumura (2018), Lin and Matsumura (2012), Matsumura and Shimizu (2010), Matsumura and Okamura (2015), and Gil-Moltó, Poyago-Theotoky, Rodrigues-Neto, and Zikos (2020).

Notice that comparing equilibrium outcomes:

(i) $q_0^M > q_i^P > q_i^M$ and

(ii) $Q^M = q_0^M + nq_i^M > (n+1)q_i^P = Q^P$.

We can therefore distinguish the following effects:

1. post-privatisation the public firm reduces its output ($q_i^P < q_0^M$),
2. post-privatisation each private firm increases its output ($q_i^P > q_i^M$),
3. privatisation decreases total output ($Q^M > Q^P$).

There is output substitution away from the public firm towards the private firms. This is a direct consequence of the public (now privatised) firm no longer maximising social welfare which was addressing the underproduction failure associated with imperfect competition. Taken together effects (1) and (3) reduce welfare while effect (2) increases welfare. Furthermore, effect (2) is stronger and effect (3) is weaker, the larger the number of private firms, n. Put in a different way, in the mixed oligopoly, despite the allocative efficiency that comes from price being equal to marginal cost, there is productive inefficiency stemming from the unequal distribution of costs. It is this latter inefficiency that dominates when there are many private firms so that $W^P > W^M$. Figure 2 illustrates the previous discussion.

The result that $W^P > W^M$ depends crucially on the temporal structure of firms interactions, as in the case of the public firm acting as a Stackelberg leader setting its output before the private firms, there is a clear case *against* privatisation.[12]

The main contribution of De Fraja and Delbono (1989) is to highlight the role of market structure in determining the optimality of privatisation in a quantity competition oligopolistic framework. While strategic interactions and cost inefficiencies may restrict the public firm from improving social welfare, as long as firms compete simultaneously it always improves efficiency with respect to a privatised market when firms compete sequentially.[13]

The second solution in order to avoid the rather unsatisfactory outcome of a public monopoly, is to consider constant marginal costs but allow for

---

[12] In earlier contributions, Harris and Wiens (1980) also argue for the superiority of Stackelberg leadership by the public firm while Beato and Mas-Colell (1984) consider the public firm as a follower. There is no justification for their choice of the order of moves, an issue taken up by a number of papers on endogenous timing (Amir & De Feo, 2014; Matsumura, 2003; D. Pal, 1998).

[13] Matsumura and Shimizu (2010) demonstrate the robustness of the results of De Fraja and Delbono (1989) by considering multiple public firms, asymmetric production costs between public and private firms, as well as product differentiation.

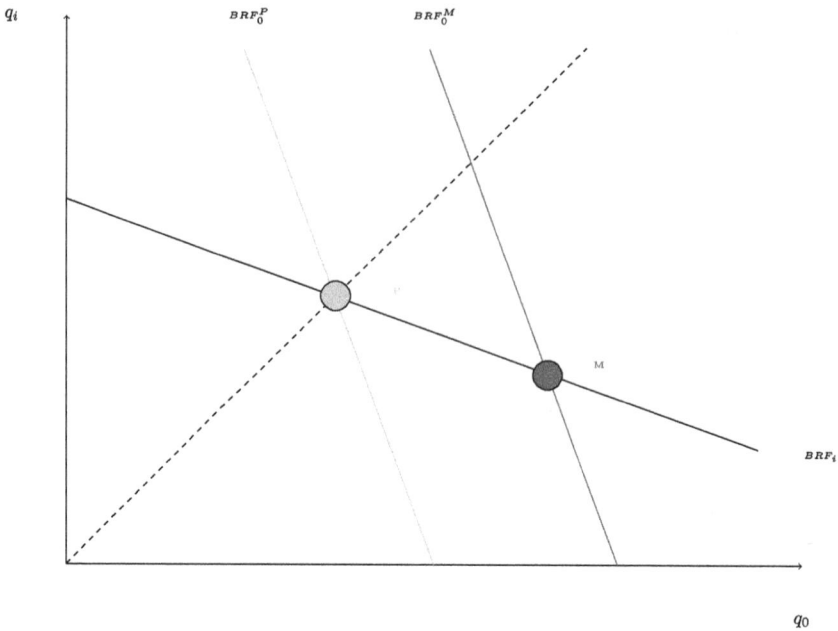

Figure 2 Private vs mixed oligopoly.
Note: BRF_i: Best-response function for a representative private firm; BRF_0^M: Best-response function of public firm, before privatisation; BRF_0^P: Best-response function of public firm, after privatisation. M: Mixed oligopoly equilibrium, P: Private oligopoly equilibrium.

cost differences. Consider the following simple duopoly in a market for a homogeneous good. Demand is linear and given by $p = a - Q$ (expression 7) with $Q = q_0 + q_1$, where q_0 is the output of the public firm and q_1 the output of its private rival. There are no fixed costs. Unit costs of production are constant and differ so that $c_0 > c_1$, with $c_0 = c$ and $c_1 = 0$; that is, the public firm is less efficient, and $a > 2c$ to ensure an interior solution. Everything else remains the same.

The mixed duopoly Nash equilibrium is then characterised by the intersection of the following best-response functions:

$$q_0(q_1) = \frac{\partial W_0}{\partial q_0} = a - c - q_1$$

$$q_1(q_0) = \frac{\partial \pi_1}{\partial q_1} = \frac{1}{2}(a - q_0),$$

yielding the solution

$$q_0 = a - 2c$$

$$q_1 = c$$

and

$$p = a - (q_0 + q_1) = c,$$

and it is evident that in this equilibrium both firms produce, price is set at marginal cost, the private firm makes a profit, $\pi_1 = c^2$, and the public firm just breaks even, $\pi_0 = 0$.

Interestingly, adding a small fixed cost would make the public firm incurring a loss. In this vein, Cremer, Marchand, and Thisse (1989) consider a homogeneous good Cournot-Nash oligopoly where $n+m$ firms operate under increasing returns (a fixed cost and constant marginal costs) and public firms face a budget constraint while their objective is to maximise total surplus. The outcome is then shown to be equivalent to a second-best solution. The benefits from the presence of more than one public firm in the market are though limited by the budget constraint which limits aggregate output expansion.

However, in the previous simple story, there is no explanation for the difference in productive efficiency (captured by the differing unit costs) which is imposed exogenously. There is no general consensus on whether a public firm is more or less efficient in its productive activities: in fact there has been a large number of empirical studies but with mixed results. It is not a priori clear that a public firm is inefficient, and hence a target for privatisation. Some studies on the relative performance of public firms conclude that they are less efficient hence favouring private sector ownership; these results are reviewed by Megginson and Netter (2001). But equally, there are other works pointing to the opposite direction, favouring public ownership; for example, see Mühlenkamp (2015) for a more recent and balanced account. Leaving aside this debate, we now offer some theoretical explanations for the discrepancy in productive efficiency.

One interpretation that we explore in more detail in Section 4.4, explains cost differences as stemming from firms' innovative activities. Alternative explanations are due to organisational or managerial slack (X-inefficiency), with De Fraja (1993) showing that the public firm may be more efficient precisely because of its social welfare objective where the government principal has 'more to gain' from a given improvement in the firm's efficiency (De Fraja, 1993, p. 17). Willner and Parker (2007) elaborate further by extending this argument by building on De Fraja (1993) and considering both demand and cost uncertainty but more importantly consider the question of entry and competition, following privatisation of the public firm. In addition, they make a distinction between active ownership (the output decision of the public firm is taken by the owner-government principal) and passive ownership (the output decision is made by the manager). In this enhanced setting they confirm that the public firm obtains lower managerial slack, while the impact of competition may lead to instances where firms are less efficient following entry.

Furthermore, De Fraja (1991) identifies the conditions for the optimality of privatisation to arise under constant marginal costs and a less efficient public firm. He focuses on the higher productive efficiency achieved by privatising a public firm (post-privatisation) and the loss of efficiency due to the output restriction induced by the presence of a profit-concerned firm in the market. By improving the productive efficiency of state-owned enterprises, privatisation enhances overall welfare. A trade-off between allocative and productive efficiency (i.e., between cost reductions and allocative gains) can be favourable to public ownership in this case. A positive net effect leading to welfare gains arises when cost differences between the public and the private firms ex ante privatisation, and consequently the efficiency gains post-privatisation, are high enough.

3 Alternative Objectives for the Public Firm

Often a public firm is not fully owned by the state; instead, the government retains a stake (controlling or not) via holding shares in a 'partly state-owned' or 'partially-privatised' firm (OECD, 2017, 2018).

In this case, additional issues emerge pertaining to the particular objective function of the quasi-public firm and to the extent of state shareholding or involvement. An ancillary, but nevertheless important, question relates to the optimal degree of privatisation of the public firm, in other words, the determination of the optimal degree of public ownership.

Consider a simple example of a mixed duopoly, following from the previous section: firm 0 is partly state-owned and firm 1 is fully private, profit-maximising. Demand is linear, given by expression (7). Both firms have identical affine cost functions, $c_i(q_i) = f + cq_i, i = 0, 1$, and, for our purposes here, we can set $f = 0$. Let $\theta \in [0, 1]$ denote the proportion of shares the government controls in firm 0, with $\theta = 0$ denoting a fully private firm and $\theta = 1$ denoting a fully public firm. Fershtman (1990), in his pioneering analysis on the role of type of ownership on entry deterrence and privatisation, introduced a family of best response functions for firm 0, directly dependent on the value of θ. In particular, when firm 0 acts as a private firm ($\theta = 0$), its best-response function is given by

$$q_0^P(q_1) = \frac{\partial \pi_0}{\partial q_0} = \frac{1}{2}(a - q_1 - c), \tag{8}$$

while when it acts as fully public ($\theta = 1$), the associated best-response function is

$$q_0^M(q_1) = \frac{\partial W_0}{\partial q_0} = (a - q_1 - c). \tag{9}$$

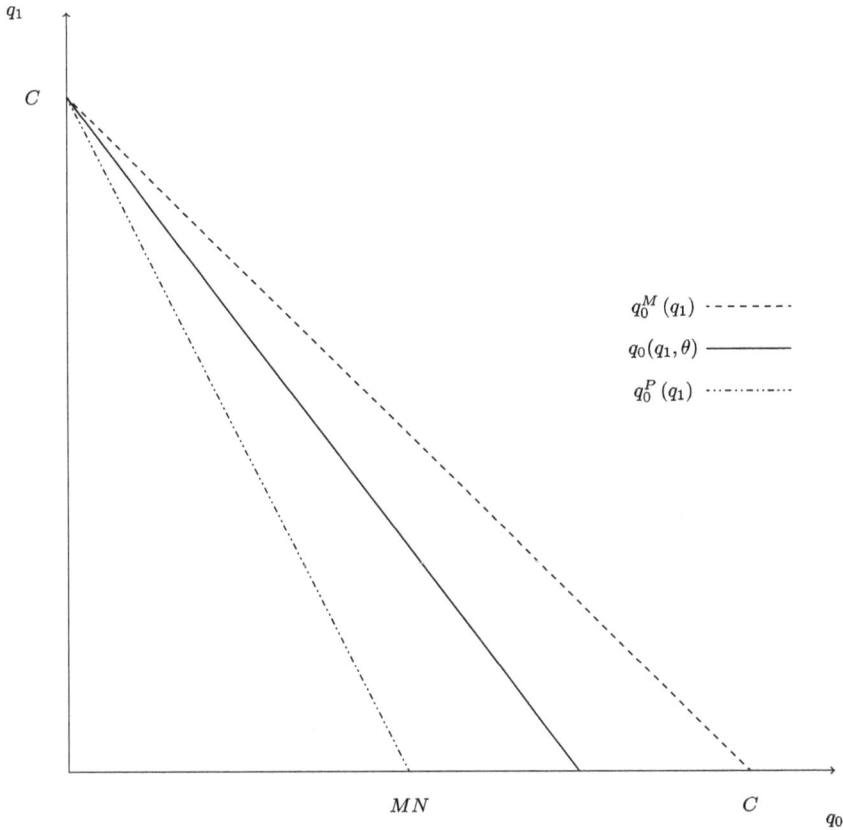

Figure 3 Best-response functions for partly state-owned firm.
Note: MN: monopoly output, C: competitive output

A simple way to represent the best-response function for firm 0 when it is partly state-owned is to take the weighted average of (8) and (9):

$$q_0(q_1, \theta) = \theta q_0^M(q_1) + (1 - \theta) q_0^P(q_1) = \frac{1}{2}(1 - \theta)(a - q_1 - c). \tag{10}$$

Figure 3 illustrates the objective function of the public firm U_0 giving rise to these best-response functions is given by:

$$U_0 = \theta W + (1 - \theta)\pi_0 \tag{11}$$

where W and π_0 are given by (4) and (3) respectively, after substituting the specific functions of this example. Expression (11) is basically the objective function for a partially privatised public firm, first introduced by Matsumura (1998) in his seminal contribution.

Matsumura (1998) uses a mixed duopoly model with general cost and demand functions and, by allowing governments to sell a share of their assets in the public firm they control to private firms, addresses the issue of partial privat-isation and juxtaposes this to full privatisation and full nationalisation. Under partial privatisation, a (partially privatised) firm is jointly owned by the pub-lic and the private sector and maximises a weighted average of social welfare and its own profits (see expression (11)). It is thus acting also in the interests of private shareholders. The optimal extent of privatisation, namely the degree of government ownership in the privatised firm, is determined as the optimal weight (optimal θ) assigned on social welfare as opposed to profits in the firm's objective function. Matsumura (1998) finds that the decision to nationalise a sector is optimal ($\theta = 1$) only under public monopoly, while full privatisation ($\theta = 0$) is never an equilibrium outcome. Moreover, with partial privatisation the semi-public firm does not price at marginal cost which allows private firms to expand output and improve allocative efficiency.

Following on from Matsumura (1998), the question of whether it is optimal to allow public firms compete against private firms together with the determin-ation of the optimal degree of public ownership within semi-public firms has become a lively topic in the mixed oligopoly literature.

The search for the optimal degree of public ownership reveals that pure welfare-maximising behaviour is never optimal in the presence of an exoge-nous number of firms. Conversely, Matsumura and Kanda (2005) show that the optimality of pure welfare maximisation is obtained when a domestic free-entry market is considered; that is, the number of private firms becomes endogen-ous.[14] Furthermore, in a variety of contexts partial privatisation depends on the strength of competition. In particular, Lin and Matsumura (2012) find that the optimal extent of privatisation increases with the number of private firms and decreases in the foreign ownership share in private firms while Mat-sumura and Okamura (2015) show that the optimal degree of privatisation under interdependent payoffs (i.e., they consider firm relative performance approach) is higher when market competition is lower and depends on firms' cost structure.[15]

More generally the analysis of the optimal extent of privatisation raises the question on the appropriate optimising behaviour of a public firm. Along this research line, there is an interesting interface and connection with the literature

---

[14] The result of Matsumura and Kanda (2005) is dependent on the presence of domestic private firms in the market. Cato and Matsumura (2012) find a positive optimal degree of privatisation in an international free-entry market. An international free-entry market is described in Lee, Matsumura, and Sato (2018), in which the degree of privatisation is determined after firms' entry.

[15] For the case of partial privatisation in vertically related markets see Chang and Ryu (2015) and Wu, Chang, and Chen (2016).

on strategic delegation in mixed markets,[16] which likewise considers firms' objectives as endogenous and provides reasons for considering pure welfare maximisation as suboptimal: social welfare increases when, through the use of incentive contracts, public managers are allowed to put some weight on profits besides social welfare only.

The theoretical analysis that deals with the decision of a public authority to partially privatise a public firm is reflected in the use of an objective function that weights welfare and profits. This is equivalent to models of strategic delegation with public firms, where an incentive contract that weights welfare and profit is offered to public managers by public owners. Therefore, partial privatisation can be interpreted as partial strategic delegation of the public firm to private managers with profit concerns, since the objective function of the mixed ownership firm is the same as the objective function of a public manager under delegation. Thus discussing a firm's optimal ownership structure amounts to considering its optimal internal structure. The strategy to partially privatise is equivalent to the strategy to delegate control, and the emphasis on profits can represent both the share of private ownership and the power of incentives (Benassi et al., 2014).

Pure welfare maximisation is not pursued by governments in circumstances in which their interests may conflict with those of public firms. For example, it does not represent the social optimum from the government's viewpoint when the latter prefers tax revenue to social welfare (Kato et al., 2008), and it is most likely not the optimal choice when governments and public firms have different objectives due to cost subsidisation of public firms (Saha, 2009). There are also potential welfare effects of a change in a public firm's objective function when a government takes into account the excess taxation burden, for example, as in Sato and Matsumura (2019), who introduce the shadow cost of public funds and find that its relationship with the optimal privatisation policy is non-monotone.

To close this section, we move away from the normative issues presented up to this point and briefly mention a distinctly different and positive approach to describing a public firm's objective. In particular, political reasons may induce governments not to advocate welfare maximisation. This is the case of the manipulation of public firms' objectives which reflects the state's attitude towards welfare, potentially biased towards consumer surplus or private

---

[16] Strategic delegation in mixed markets has been introduced by Barros (1994) in a duopoly quantity setting and then extended to oligopoly (Heywood & Ye, 2009a), price competition with endogenous timing (Nakamura & Inoue, 2009), and international trade (Chang, 2007). A different strand of this literature relates to social economy enterprises (co-ops, mutuals, charities, etc.). For interesting and detailed analyses of strategic delegation in consumer cooperatives see, amongst others, Kopel, Lamantia, and Szidarovszky (2014); Kopel and Marini (2012, 2014).

profits (White, 2002). The nature of interactions with private firms is such that a government can strategically assign an objective function to the public firm in order to disguise their real political orientation. White (2002) highlights how delegation can be used by governments as a device through which they maximise their true objective by allowing the public firm to maximise a different objective function. Such a strategy enables a government to pursue unpopular programs, in fact disguising their actual motives.

4 A Smorgasbord of Applications

In this section, we present a selective account of a number of applications and extensions of the basic ideas and models introduced thus far. In particular, we pay attention to a series of results on the 'irrelevance' of the nature of market setups, when a policy of output subsidisation is used to address the under-production market failure associated with imperfect competition. Next we briefly overview contributions in industrial organisation, open economies and international competition and, finally, research and development (R&D) and close with a brief mentioning of banking competition.

4.1 'Irrelevance' Results–Privatisation Neutrality Theorem (PNT)

Recent literature on mixed markets has dealt with the issue of optimal subsidies provided to public and private firms in a mixed oligopoly with the aim of achieving maximum welfare. The common thread is the 'irrelevance' of firm ownership (public or private) when firms are given uniform production subsidies which succeed in restoring the first-best allocation. Subsidisation, therefore, gives rise to the *privatisation neutrality theorem* (PNT), which basically states that the equilibrium output, firms' profits, and social welfare are identical before and after privatisation. In the mixed oligopoly, the subsidy contributes to overall efficiency due to cost distribution effects.[17]

This irrelevance result and associated PNT was first uncovered by White (1996), who considered a simultaneous move oligopoly with quantity competition, linear demand and quadratic costs. Assigning to the public firm the role of Stackelberg leader does not change this result (Poyago-Theotoky, 2001), which is also confirmed for general demand and cost functions (Myles et al., 2002). However, when the public leader keeps the leadership

---

[17] The privatisation neutrality theorem (PNT) in this section is to be distinguished from a different 'irrelevance theorem', or 'fundamental theorem of privatisation', introduced by Sappington and Stiglitz (1987) and formalised by Martimort (2006). The latter theorem, developed in an incentive theoretical framework, states that privatisation, under some conditions, may be an optimal solution to the delegation problem and replicates what can be achieved with public production.

position post-privatisation (Fjell & Heywood, 2004), or if there are foreign competitors in the market (Matsumura & Tomaru, 2012), the irrelevance result no longer holds. It continues to hold under price competition and differentiated products (Hashimzade et al., 2007) and when private firms maximise a weighted average of own profits and some other factor (Kato & Tomaru, 2007).

Optimal subsidisation in mixed markets has been revisited in the context of partial privatisation. The irrelevance of partial privatisation (i.e., equilibrium output, firms' profits and social welfare are identical regardless of the share of public ownership in the state-controlled firm) has been demonstrated under simultaneous moves in a Cournot competitive scenario (Tomaru et al., 2006) and in a setting comparing price and quantity competition (Scrimitore, 2014). In contrast, Tomaru and Wang (2018) and Lin and Matsumura (2018) suggest that the PNT never holds in the presence of a cost gap between public and private firms.

Two caveats are in order. First, the general acceptance and applicability of output subsidies as a policy tool; and second, the potential of non-uniform, that is, discriminatory, subsidies. Output subsidies can be a controversial policy as international organisations such as the International Monetary Fund (IMF) and the World Trade Organisation (WTO) have traditionally viewed them rather unfavourably. Thus a related question concerns the use of alternative subsidisation policies, such as R&D subsidies which are less controversial and widely used. In general, the PNT does not survive intact in this situation (Gil-Moltó et al., 2020; Gil-Moltó et al., 2011). Moreover, when the PNT does not hold when uniform subsidies are in use, one way to restore it consists in employing discriminatory subsidies. Using asymmetric subsidies, Zikos (2007) recovers 'irrelevance' in the public leadership post-privatisation case explored by Fjell and Heywood (2004), while Hamada (2016) extends White (1996) for the case of firms facing different costs. For the case of general objectives (other than welfare maximisation) for the public firm and general demand and costs, Hamada (2018) establishes how the use of discriminatory subsidies ensure privatisation neutrality but in limited cases.

4.2 Industrial Organisation

A significant body of the literature on mixed oligopoly largely rests on the assumption that firms compete with respect to quantities (Cournot), while a relatively fewer number of works assume that firms compete with respect to prices (Bertrand).[18] Among these, Ogawa et al. (2006) investigate the role

---

[18] There is a long tradition in industrial organisation on the appropriate modelling choice for an oligopoly. See the surveys by Shapiro (1989) and Tremblay and Tremblay (2019).

of price competition in both simultaneous and sequential move settings under decreasing returns to scale. Anderson, De Palma, and Thisse (1997) analyse the case of a domestic mixed market under monopolistic competition and argue that privatisation is welfare-reducing while Matsumura, Matsushima, and Ishibashi (2009) extend this to the presence of foreign firms.

Ghosh and Mitra (2010), by performing a comparison between Cournot and Bertrand competition in mixed markets under constant marginal costs and product differentiation, highlight the peculiar features of strategic interactions in a Bertrand mixed market and contribute to a better understanding of how the mode of competition affects the equilibrium outcome. They show that, in a market with a welfare-maximising firm, consumer surplus is higher under Cournot than under Bertrand, which contrasts with the well-known result of Singh and Vives (1984) that in a private market price competition benefits consumers more than quantity competition. Their result is driven by the higher aggressiveness of the public firm under Cournot competition which lowers market prices, thus benefitting consumers, to a higher extent than under Bertrand competition. However, softer competition in Bertrand compared to Cournot results in social welfare being higher in the former, since firms' higher profits overcome the reduction in consumer surplus.[19]

In the context of partial privatisation, Fujiwara (2007) considers a standard model of differentiated goods and explores the welfare consequences of partially privatising the public firm and highlights the role of consumers' preference of variety (or, product substitutability) in determining the optimal degree of privatisation.

Moving on to applications in spatial competition (address models of product differentiation, where the 'address' refers to either physical location or product characteristics), Cremer, Marchand, and Thisse (1991) introduced public firms into a standard Hotelling model of horizontal differentiation with quadratic transport costs and showed that social welfare is higher in a mixed duopoly as the public firm chooses to locate optimally on the line to minimise transport costs and thus maximise surplus. Their approach has been further developed in several directions such as: sequential location (Matsumura & Matsushima, 2003), spatial agglomeration (Matsushima & Matsumura, 2003), spatial price discrimination (Heywood & Ye, 2009b; Matsushima & Matsumura, 2006), and endogenous cost differences (Matsushima & Matsumura, 2004).

---

[19] See also Haraguchi and Matsumura (2016) for an extensions to $n + 1$ firms, Hirose and Matsumura (2019) on the effect of Stackelberg leadership by either the private or the public firm, and Matsumura and Ogawa (2012) for complementary goods.

In general, the results obtained are sensitive to the underlying assumptions so that there is no clear consensus on the superiority or not of public firms in regulating activity in a mixed market, pointing to the need for solid empirical investigations.

4.3 Open Economies and International Competition

Privatisation waves started in Europe in the 1980s in many sectors, such as network industries (telecommunications, transport, energy, utilities), banking and insurance, postal services, education, and health. These sectors have also been increasingly exposed to international competition, in response to international liberalisation and globalisation. In this sense, the concept of mixed oligopoly can be applied to throw light on the interaction of public firms (fully public or partially privatised) in the context of international competition, bridging the fields of international trade theory with industrial organisation.

In this context a key issue arises in distinguishing between market interactions within a country (single country approach), and interactions across countries (two-country approach). While the former are related to the operation of firms (public and private) characterised by different motives and to the contribution of foreign firms to domestic welfare and effect on competition within the home market, the latter concern international competition and its effects stemming from governments' strategic interactions.

The extent to which the competitive pressure exerted by private foreign firms alters competition in a mixed domestic market is a common theme. Within the single-country approach, the presence of foreign private competitors on the domestic market has been shown to affect the optimal privatisation policy (Chang, 2005; Chao & Yu, 2006; Matsumura & Tomaru, 2012), market opening and cross-border acquisitions (Fjell & Pal, 1996), strategic trade policy (Pal & White, 1998; Van Long & Stähler, 2009), as well as productive efficiency of the public firm (Tomaru, 2007). Moreover, the two-country approach has been used to investigate the extent to which interactions between governments affect unilateral or coordinated privatisation (Dadpay & Heywood, 2006), strategic privatisation (Bárcena-Ruiz & Garzón, 2005b), the optimal degree of privatisation (Han, 2012; Han & Ogawa, 2008), strategic trade policy (Bárcena-Ruiz & Garzón, 2005a; Pal & White, 2003), and the interplay of privatisation and foreign direct investment (Dijkstra et al., 2015; Mukherjee & Suetrong, 2009).

In one of the earliest contributions, Corneo and Jeanne (1994) considered a common (integrated) market consisting of many countries where public and private firms produce a homogeneous good, with some countries not having a public firm. The objective of a public firm is adjusted to reflect concern with the domestic economy only, so that a public firm maximises total surplus in the national economy as opposed to the integrated market, and can be expressed uniquely in terms of exports. They find a unique Cournot equilibrium where countries with a public firm are net exporters. More recently, Willner, Grönblom, Kainu, and Flink (2018), within a two-country intra-industry trade setup, question the effect foreign competitors have on the inclusion of nonprofit elements in the objective function of a state-owned firm in a setting where labour costs and mobility play a role. In particular, they ask, 'whether the weight for non-profit objectives (here the consumer surplus) has to become lower or if it even must become zero in an open economy' (Willner et al., 2018, p. 416). It turns out that the answer is nuanced and the scope of nonprofit objectives is curtailed and depends on cost conditions, the relative size of a country, and whether firms and workers are stationary.

Finally, in one of the very few papers cast in a general equilibrium framework, Ghosh and Sen (2012) examine the feasibility and welfare effects of privatisation in a small (developing) economy under imperfect competition and tariffs. They interpret privatisation as a reduction in public firms' production and find that although it may improve welfare via an increase in tariff revenue it may also decrease welfare via a decrease in wage rates and product variety. Hence they argue that for privatisation to be politically feasible it has to be combined with additional complementary reforms, such as trade liberalisation and FDI.

4.4 Research and Development–R&D

Given a broader interpretation, a public firm can encompass publicly funded R&D laboratories, scientific nonprofit institutions, university labs, and state-owned enterprises engaged in R&D.

Several market failures afflict the innovation process stemming from the public good nature of knowledge and information. When there are no involuntary leakages of information, that is, spillovers are absent, perhaps as a result of a very effective patent system or conditions of stringent secrecy, firms tend to overinvest in R&D in their attempt to gain an advantage over their rivals. This is a strategic overinvestment effect. In contrast, when there are involuntary leakages of information, that is, there are positive spillovers, then the larger the spillover the smaller the incentive for R&D so that firms underinvest in R&D. This is the familiar appropriability problem which gives rise to a strategic underinvestment effect. Both the strategic overinvestment effect and the strategic underinvestment effect are manifestations of an R&D market failure: for a variety of reasons firms choose the wrong level of R&D relative to the social optimum. Hence there is room for policy intervention where a public firm can influence innovative activity and address the innovation market failure.

Typically, R&D competition between firms is modelled either as a tournament or as a non-tournament model. In a tournament model of R&D, or patent race, there can only be one winner who takes all the rewards associated with a new process or product with the profit motive guiding firms to overinvest. Having a public firm operate alongside the private firm(s), because it is not profit-oriented, results in each firm reducing investment in R&D, and an increase in social welfare (Delbono & Denicolo, 1993). However, this result is obtained when imitation is not possible due to strong patent protection. Often though imitation is easy, with creators of innovations more often than not finding it difficult to appropriate fully the returns from their R&D investment.[20] Within this context and using a waiting game, Poyago-Theotoky (1998) shows that a public firm can be useful as a regulatory instrument that tackles the underinvestment in R&D, as it is not affected by the free-rider problem. Innovation size or technological choice are the focus of I. Ishibashi and Matsumura (2006), who examine competition in R&D between a public research institute and a private firm and find that the public firm (institute) opts for an innovation size too small while R&D spending is higher relative to social optimum. They thus argue against privatisation.

In line with the question on the productive efficiency of public versus private firms, there is also the associated question of which type of firm, public or private, is more innovative, in other words, what effect does a difference in organisational goals have on innovative activity.[21]

This question is better answered in the context of non-tournament models of R&D competition, where firms are not engaged in a race but can all succeed at the same time in generating an innovation, as there are several, distinct but equivalent paths, to an innovation. Thus, in the absence of spillovers, Nett (1994) considers a mixed duopoly, where the public firm maximises output with a zero-budget constraint, and both firms decide whether to invest in a process innovation with a fixed cost and then compete in output. Because of the aggressive behaviour of the public firm that stems from output maximisation, the private firm invests more in R&D to compensate and thus operate with

---

[20]　See Levin et al. (1987) for an early and very influential contribution.

[21]　Public firms are key players in highly R&D-intensive sectors such as healthcare, bio-agriculture, and energy (see, e.g., Oehmke (2001), Godø, Nerdrum, Rapmund, and Nygaard (2003); Godø and Nygaard (2006). This is not a recent occurrence; for example, Malerba (1993) reports that in Italy, from the 1960s through to the 1980s, there have been two public firms in the top R&D investors. A more recent approach views the public firm as mission-oriented in creating and fostering radical innovation; for example, see Castelnovo and Florio (2020) for a detailed account also covering empirical evidence on SOEs innovation activities.

lower unit costs, it is more efficient than the public firm. However, introducing spillovers, Zhang and Zhong (2015) reverse this result for relatively strong spillovers and show that the public firm is more innovative. This latter result is echoed in Heywood and Ye (2009c) for a mixed duopoly with a partially privatised public firm, maximising a combination of profits and welfare, as in (11), and complete spillovers.

Interestingly, the policy-relevant issues of R&D subsidies in the context of mixed oligopolies have not been explored extensively, in clear contrast to the key role of R&D subsidisation and the role of public firms in facilitating innovation and the development of national innovation systems. In this context, the role of spillovers and the desirability of privatisation are explored in Gil-Moltó et al. (2011) within a setting of a mixed duopoly where the public firm is maximising social welfare and both firms receive R&D subsidies. The socially optimal R&D increases in the spillover rate and is higher in the mixed market, whereas privatisation is welfare-reducing and results in a reduction of R&D.

Gil-Moltó et al. (2020) extend Gil-Moltó et al. (2011) to an oligopoly, comprising n private firms and one public firm and, using aggregative-game techniques, confirm that privatisation reduces the optimal R&D subsidy but, more importantly, privatisation improves social welfare when n is large, the latter result being in line with De Fraja and Delbono (1989) who do not consider R&D. This latter result suggests that pursuing a policy of privatisation may be socially desirable as long as the number of private firms is sufficiently large. A further policy implication relates to the design of R&D subsidisation programmes, advocating careful consideration of the number of firms in a given industry, as there are instances were a suitable tax on R&D implements the maximal welfare.[22]

4.5 Banking Competition

In an influential paper, La Porta, Lopez-de Silanes, and Shleifer (2002) provide evidence on government ownership of banks worldwide and state that it is substantial and pervasive, accounting for about 41.6 per cent (38.5 per cent if former socialist countries are excluded) in 1995. They also argue that there is mostly a negative relationship between government ownership and economic growth. This conclusion is challenged by Andrianova, Demetriades, and Shortland (2012), who present new cross-country evidence with data for 1995–2007, and conclude that, on the contrary, government ownership of banks results in

---

[22] See also Zikos (2010) for an analysis of endogenous network formation to examine the incentives for R&D collaboration in a mixed oligopoly.

higher long-run growth. Moreover, following the great financial crisis (GFC) of 2008, several governments, in order to prevent financial meltdown, took large stakes in major commercial banks (e.g., the rescue of the Royal Bank of Scotland by the UK government). Furthermore, the recent collapse of Credit Suisse in March 2023 and the discussions on whether it should become a government controlled bank (Bris, 2023) point to the increased role of government in the banking sector.

Surprisingly, despite this evidence, there is rather little research exploring the interaction between private and public banks and financial institutions. Yet, it seems that the concept and analytical apparatus of mixed oligopoly represents a suitable tool for exploring this interaction: in several instances, the banking sector appears to be a mixed oligopoly. Barros and Modesto (1999) is one of the earliest papers to establish that the banking sector resembles a mixed oligopoly (in the loan market), presenting a simple theoretical model that underlies their empirical analysis of the Portuguese banking sector.

The literature on mixed oligopoly and banking is still tentative and incomplete. Obviously, this is an area where further research is needed. There are basically two issues that have been addressed: (i) deposit competition (Saha & Sensarma, 2011) and (ii) loan competition (Bose et al., 2014; Saha & Sensarma, 2013). Saha and Sensarma (2011) focus on the interplay of managerial incentives provided by the private bank and the extent of privatisation of the public bank, using a mixed duopoly model where the two banks compete in the collection of deposits. In the case of lending, there is concern for the associated credit risk of loans, and this has an impact on deposits and associated losses of depositors. In this setting, Saha and Sensarma (2013) find that when credit risk is sufficiently high and there is limited liability, the public (or partially private) bank alleviates depositors' losses by mobilising less deposits so that there is a contraction of total deposits. The increase in government ownership of banks and its effect on lenders behaviour are closely examined in Bose et al. (2014), who identify perverse instances where lender profit can increase. Recently Andolfatto (2021) addresses the question of the introduction of central bank digital currency (CBDC) and its impact on the banking sector for the case of a monopolised banking sector and finds that a CBDC has no detrimental effect on lending, whereas Chiu, Davoodalhosseini, Jiang, and Zhu (2019) consider a Cournot oligopoly.

5 Current Issues

In this section we present what we believe are some important current issues, which are also worthy of additional research: quality provision, including health providers' competition and education, environmental aspects, and the role of intrinsic motivation in public firms.

5.1 Quality Provision and Mixed Markets

Public firms often operate in markets for goods or services where quality is important and the main characteristic of the good or service provided. This is especially the case in the provision of health services, education, and transport amongst others. Many of these markets are regulated, so the role of the public firm becomes multifaceted. In these markets, competition takes place primarily along the quality dimension, so we need to consider the basics of competition in this context. The way to do so is by looking at vertical differentiation models and their adaptation to mixed oligopolistic markets.

To begin with, most people agree that higher quality is preferable; there is an agreement on the preference ordering by all concerned: if these goods or services were to be offered for sale at identical prices, every consumer would rank them in the same order. In its simplest form, we capture this as follows:

Suppose the quality characteristic of the good/service is represented by a number $s_i \in [\underline{s}, \overline{s}] \subset \mathcal{R}_+$. Consumers' preferences are described by a quasi-linear utility function,

$$U = \vartheta s - p$$

if a consumer buys one unit of quality s and pays a price p and $U = 0$ if he does not buy. There is heterogeneity in how consumers value quality, although they all agree that higher quality is better. Let $\vartheta \in [\underline{\vartheta}, \overline{\vartheta}] \subset \mathcal{R}_+$ capture this heterogeneity. The quality parameter ϑ is a random variable with distribution F and strictly positive density f and is continuously differentiable. Most papers on vertical differentiation and mixed oligopoly use the uniform distribution.[23] In particular, the parameter ϑ is uniformly distributed over $[\underline{\vartheta}, \overline{\vartheta}]$, $\overline{\vartheta} > \underline{\vartheta} > 0$, so that $f(\vartheta) = \frac{1}{\overline{\vartheta} - \underline{\vartheta}}$ and without loss of generality one can set $\overline{\vartheta} - \underline{\vartheta} = 1$.

Next assume there are two firms, firm 1 and firm 2, charging price p_i, for a good of quality $s_i, i = 1, 2$. Firm 1 is public and maximises social welfare, $W = CS + \pi_1 + \pi_2$, while firm 2 is private and maximises profit, π_2.

An important concept is the notion of a covered versus a non-covered market. In the former, each consumer buys one of the two qualities on offer; in the latter some consumers do not buy at all. This distinction has implications for the derivation of demands and hence firms' objective functions and subsequent results.

---

[23] Notable exceptions are Benassi, Castellani, and Mussoni (2016) and Laine and Ma (2017) who use general distributions as well as providing examples using the Pareto distribution (Benassi et al., 2016) and the triangular, truncated exponential and beta distributions (Laine & Ma, 2017).

In a covered market, $D_1(p_1,p_2) + D_2(p_1,p_2) = 1$, whereas in an uncovered market, $D_1(p_1,p_2) + D_2(p_1,p_2) < 1$, $D_i(p_1,p_2) > 0$, where $D_i(p_1,p_2)$ represents the demand for good/service $i = 1,2$ given prices, p_1 and p_2.

In general, an oligopolistic market does not achieve social optimality as there is underprovision of quality (Moorthy, 1988). Here too, a public firm can be used as a policy instrument to restore optimality as shown by Grilo (1994), one of the earliest contributions on quality and mixed duopoly. A mixed duopoly with vertical differentiation is analysed where two equally efficient firms, one private and one public, compete in setting the quality and then the price of their respective products. The objective of the public firm is to maximise total surplus under a non-negative budget constraint. Although unit costs of production are constant, they are increasing in quality. The notion of quality preference is captured by a uniform distribution describing consumers' willingness to pay for a better product. Given full market coverage Grilo (1994) finds that the social optimum can be restored.

An issue not answered directly in Grilo (1994) relates to whether the public firm offers a higher- or lower-quality product than its private counterpart. Often the product or service provided by a public firm is of lower quality, for example, healthcare, postal services, especially when such a product has to reach as many consumers as possible (universal obligation). K. Ishibashi and Kaneko (2008), using a Hotelling-type setup, show that in a simple mixed duopoly the public firm underprovides while the private firm overprovides quality. By allowing for partial privatisation of the public firm, a better quality allocation can be achieved but not the first-best, as there is only one policy instrument, the degree of privatisation chosen by the government, to correct for several market failures. The optimal degree of privatisation depends on the extent of market competition captured by the extent of transportation costs. Interpreting higher quality in terms of environmental cleanliness, in a covered market, Nabin, Nguyen, Sgro, and Chao (2014) argue for the superiority of public monopoly as opposed to either partial or full privatisation as private or semi-public firms fail to take properly account of environmental externalities.

By contrast, in an uncovered market where some consumers do not buy the good at all, with similar quality costs but in a purely vertical differentiation model similar to Grilo (1994), Lutz and Pezzino (2014) consider a 'semi-public' firm which maximises welfare in the long run, that is, only when setting quality. Again, the mixed duopoly outperforms the private one irrespective of whether the public firm provides the high- or low-quality good. Perception of quality is captured by using the uniform distribution which, although analytically convenient, cannot account for inequality affecting the willingness to pay for quality. To partly remedy this Benassi et al. (2016) consider a general distribution and provide the conditions needed for the existence and uniqueness of a short-run price equilibrium for the case where the public firm provides the low quality. They show that existence requires the distribution of the willingness to pay must not be logconcave. In a two-stage setup with quality chosen first before price, Laine and Ma (2017) go further by establishing the conditions on consumers' quality-valuation distribution for efficient outcomes to occur in the multiple mixed duopoly equilibria they identify. In some equilibria the public firm provides the low quality, and in some this is reversed. The conditions needed for efficiency are expressed by either a linear inverse hazard rate for consumers' valuation of quality (public firm offers the low quality) or a linear inverse reverse hazard rate (public firm offers the high quality), which are quite special but satisfied by the uniform distribution (cf. Grilo (1994)). Finally, using a different approach and allowing for income heterogeneity in consumers, Klumpp and Su (2019) examine the distributional effects of policies that affect the price or quality of the public firm's product, where the public firm provides the lower-quality/low-price good.

Table 1 summarises the main theoretical findings of this section.

5.1.1 Hospital Competition and Health Provision Services

The application of product differentiation models to analyse issues of quality within a mixed oligopolistic setup has generated a new interest in its usefulness to examine competition in the quasi-market for the provision of health services, including hospital competition. There are additional features, such as regulated prices and different co-payment schemes, which can be addressed rather satisfactorily in the analytical structure of a mixed oligopoly.[24]

Jofre-Bonet (2000) is one of the earliest applications of a quality differentiation model on healthcare provision under universal coverage such that patients of low income can always access health services in the form of a basic package (this is the 'low' quality good). A provider duopoly is examined in the spirit of Sutton (1991) with increasing quality costs. Consumers-patients differ in their incomes, high or low, and the two providers choose entry, quality, and then quantity/extent of provision of services. Jofre-Bonet (2000) distinguishes between a fully private duopoly, a mixed duopoly, and fully public provision. In the mixed scenario, the private provider offers the high quality and the public provider serves the low-quality demand segment, while there is welfare improvement relative to the fully private provision, and in addition

---

[24] See www.kff.org/other/state-indicator/hospitals-by-ownership/ for information on the types of hospitals (local, state, nonprofits, profit) in the United States.

Table 1 General models–vertical differentiation.

Models	First best	puf 'strategy'	Covered market	Distribution	Comments
1: 2-stages: quality then p, equally efficient firms (Grilo, 1994)	Yes	choose welfare maximising SPE p and quality subject to non-negative profit constraint	Yes	uniform	costs increasing in quality
2: 2-stages: quality then p (K. Ishibashi & Kaneko, 2008)	No	choose SPE quality and price maximising weighted sum of SW and Π	yes	uniform	fixed (convex) costs of quality; puf provides lower quality than prf, Hotelling-type setting
3: 2-stages: quality then p (or q) (Lutz & Pezzino, 2014)	no	chooses SPE quality to maximise welfare and p (or q) to maximise profit	no	uniform	fixed quality costs; puf provides high or low quality
4: p competition, constant (zero) MC, puf low quality (Benassi et al., 2016)	no	puf chooses welfare maximising p	no	general	zero costs of production, costless quality
5: two-stage: quality then p (Laine & Ma, 2017)	yes	chooses quality and price at SPE, sets price s.t. $\Delta p = \Delta qual$	yes	general	equally efficient firms

Note: puf: public firm, p: price, q: quantity, MC: marginal cost, SPE: subgame-perfect equilibrium this is less costly. The objective function of the public provider is slightly different, as it consists of maximising consumer surplus and is subject to three constraints, namely, universal coverage, budget balance, and ensuring that the private provider breaks even.

Sanjo (2009) takes a different approach and focuses on the effect of uncertainly on the part of patients perception of quality of provision. In particular, a partially privatised public provider competes with a profit-maximising one in a Hotelling-type spatial competition setup. He finds that the public provider may offer a higher quality; this is so when patients have a high preference for quality.

In a similar Hotelling-type setup with regulated prices, Herr (2011) explores competition between a public and a private hospital, in the absence of uncertainty, but more importantly introduces a variation of the objective function of the public hospital: it maximises a linear combination of its profits and market share (output of health services).[25] This change in the objective function plus cost efficiency differentials accounts for differing results to Sanjo (2009). In particular, she finds that although the mixed duopoly may result in higher welfare when the public firm is more efficient and competition is intense, privatising the public firm may be welfare-improving when firms/hospitals are of similar efficiency and competition is contained.

The issue of opening up the healthcare market to for-profit providers is taken up by Hehenkamp and Kaarbøe (2020), who allow for entry by a private hospital provider and ask how increased competition will affect social welfare, hospital quality and the location choice of the private entrant. They do so in a Hotelling-type mixed duopoly with both horizontal and vertical differentiation and regulated prices. The objective function for the public hospital exhibits altruistic preferences in that it is a linear combination of profit and patients utility. Opening up the market in general raises quality, but at the same time the private entrant will locate towards the edge of the market to soften quality competition. Whether social welfare improves depends on the extent of altruism as well as the regulator's budget so that a mixed duopoly might not be socially preferred to a public monopoly.

Moving beyond duopoly, Ghandour and Straume (2020) present a very stylised model with three agents/hospitals, but all are heterogeneous: one hospital is fully public (welfare maximising), one is private but receives public funding, one is private but receives no public funding. The first two operate under a regulated price, while the third one sets its own price for treatment services.

---

[25] This objective function is reminiscent of the one used by Merrill and Schneider (1966) where the public firm maximises output subject to a budget constraint.

However, all three are choosing their quality. Competition is modelled along a Salop circle, where hospitals are located equidistantly, and the size of transportation cost captures the intensity of competition. They explore how the setting of the co-payment rate of the funding scheme together with the degree of competition determines the quality provision of the three providers and find that (i) a higher regulated price or co-payment rate reduces the quality provision of the public provider and increases the quality of at least one of the private providers, (ii) more intense competition improves the quality of the publicly funded private hospital.

A further application relates to competition in healthcare by for-profit and nonprofit providers as distinct from public providers (Stenbacka & Tombak, 2020). Similar to Jofre-Bonet (2000) in terms of the organisational structure of the providers, providers choose quality first and then set the price of the treatment and then patients choose where to get the treatment if at all. Stenbacka and Tombak (2020) find that in the mixed duopoly the nonprofit provides the standard quality, the for-profit the premium quality, and the market is fully covered; that is, all patients are fully served. However, there is a reversal in the identity of the quality provider, when the quality difference is relative small and the costs of upgrading quality contained, but in this latter case some patients remain unserved. The mixed duopoly outperforms other configurations in terms of social welfare due to the softening of competition. Note that the objective function for the nonprofit is the maximisation of user surplus, that is, the aggregate utility of patients served, subject to a (binding) constraint.

Table 2 presents the main characteristics of the papers of this section.

5.1.2 Further Applications

It appears then that the mixed oligopoly framework is a useful tool and framework in analysing quality issues in several areas where public provision of goods and services, such as merit goods, has been, and still is, widespread. Here we briefly consider further applications to education, schools and universities, as well as transport and postal services.

An interesting application is provided by Brunello and Rocco (2008) on schools' choice of educational standards. They present a simple model with one private and one public school, where: in stage 1 the government sets the standard for the public school, then in stage 2 the private school enters the market and sets the tuition fee and its educational standard (which can be above or below the one set by the government for the public school). They consider two different objectives/decision criteria for the public school: majority voting or a utilitarian welfare function, while the private school maximises profit. They

Table 2 Applications–healthcare provision.

Models	puf objective	model type	Comments
1: 3-stages: entry; quality; output (Jofre-Bonet, 2000)	max consumer surplus s.t. 3 constraints	pd à la Sutton (1991)	puf provides low quality
2: quality competition, uncertainty (Sanjo, 2009)	max weighted average of SW and π	Hotelling type, fixed locations	puf may offer high quality
3: 2-stages: regulated price; quality (Herr, 2011)	max weighted average of profits and market share	Hotelling type, fixed locations	different cost efficiency
4: puf incumbent; entry by prf; quality competition (Hehenkamp & Kaarbøe, 2020)	max weighted average of profit and patients' utility plus profit constraint	Hotelling type	puf has semi-altruistic preferences
5: 2-stages: quality; price (Ghandour & Straume, 2020)	max welfare	Salop circle, fixed locations	triopoly: one puf and two prf
6: quality; price; location competition (Stenbacka & Tombak, 2020)	npf max total surplus (plus constraint)	vertical diff	specifically nonprofit as opposed to puf

Note: puf: public firm, prf: private firm, npf: nonprofit firm derive two possible equilibria: the private school can choose either a higher or a lower standard. Given this, they then use empirical evidence to calibrate the parameters of the model and find that the outcome depends on the public school's objective and country where it is located. In particular:

> using empirical evidence from the US and Italy . . . find that majority voting selects low quality public school – high quality private school in the former country and low quality private school – high quality public school in the latter country. Interestingly, the choice made by majority voting turns out to be the same taken by a social planner who maximises the welfare of all the households in the economy. We interpret the difference in standards between public and private schools in these two countries as two different equilibria in our model of educational standards. (Brunello & Rocco, 2008)

Considering the effect of peer-group effects, Cremer and Maldonado (2013) examine a mixed oligopoly where schools set their quality first and then decide on tuition fees. In the absence of peer-group effects, a mixed duopoly provides an efficient outcome while a triopoly with a single public school yields lower welfare than the fully private equilibrium. When peer effects are present, the mixed oligopoly configuration is never efficient. Interestingly and somehow unexpectedly, peer-group effects reduce the power of a public school to act as a regulatory instrument.

Moving on to applications in the higher education sector, we single out the contributions of Oliveira (2006) and Lahmandi-Ayed et al. (2021). Oliveira (2006) considers university competition in the setting of admission standards, where the public university maximises welfare. The results point to different asymmetric equilibria, echoing the findings of Brunello and Rocco (2008) for the case of school standards. In a different setting, linking the higher education sector to the productive economy via skilled workers (the link is underlined by the quality of education provided within a successive monopolies framework–university and firm), Lahmandi-Ayed et al. (2021) make the case for the optimality of a partially privatised university, except for the case of high inefficiency when full privatisation is preferred.

An early paper by Cremer, De Rycke, and Grimaud (1997) examines the role of a public operator in the provision of postal services under the universal service obligation. The cost of sending a letter depends on 'quality', such as speed of delivery, with quality of service being an endogenous variable. The mixed duopoly, where the public operator maximising welfare competes with a private one, attains first-best in quality provision provided that the budget constraint is not binding. But even in the case where the budget constraint is binding, the mixed duopoly outperforms the fully private setup.

Finally, Cantos-Sánchez and Moner-Colonques (2006) present one of the few theoretical models on mixed oligopoly in the transport sector by specifically analysing two service characteristics (frequency and quality), thus combining vertical and horizontal product differentiation. In addition there is transport mode competition, for example, train versus bus, and price competition. They find that although a mixed duopoly does not recover the socially optimal solution, nevertheless it improves on the fully private scenario. It would be worthwhile to further this line of research and combine it with questions of environmental impact and market structure of the transport sector.

5.2 Environmental Aspects

Recently an area that has enjoyed a considerable revival relates to the optimal design of environmental policies, for example, the use of emission taxes, standards and permits, and in particular on the role (beneficial or not) of public firms. The framework of mixed oligopoly is used in this strand of literature to examine the effects of privatisation (or corporatisation and partial privatisation) as opposed or in conjunction with other policy instruments in a given industry. The traditional analysis (see Sections 2 and 3) is extended to include environmental effects, to show that the presence of even a single public firm internalising the environmental externalities and competing with profit-oriented private firms can be beneficial and under certain conditions suffices to restore the first-best (Lambertini, 2013, p. 209).

The main changes in the canonical model relate to incorporating the environmental context in the objective functions of the public and private firms as well as in the representation of social welfare. To illustrate for the case where the environmental policy tool is an emission tax,[26] suppose that there are n private firms and one public firm, denoted by 0, producing a homogeneous good. The inverse market demand is given by $p = p(Q)$, $p'(Q) < 0$ and $p''(Q) \leq 0$ (with $Q = q_0 + \sum_{i=1}^{n}$), where q_i, $i = 0, 1, \ldots n$, is the quantity produced by firm i. All firms share the same production technology, $c(q_i)$, $c'(q_i) > 0$ and $c''(q_i) \geq 0$. Production generates pollution, which is taxed at the rate t on emissions, while firm i can lower its tax burden by undertaking abatement activities, a_i, to reduce its emissions, at a cost of $z(a_i)$, $z'(a_i) > 0$, $z''(a_i) \geq 0$. Emissions per firm are given by $e_i = \max[q_i - a_i, 0]$ so that the emission tax per firm is te_i and total tax receipts, $T = t \sum_{i=0}^{n} e_i$. It follows that the profit function for firm i is given by

$$\pi_i = p(Q)q_i - c(q_i) - z(a_i) - te_i, i = 0, 1, \ldots n.$$

---

[26] The main framework can be adjusted to deal with market-based instruments (permits, subsidies) and command-and-control ones (standards, quotas, etc.).

Pollution is represented by total emissions, $E = \sum_{i=0}^{n} e_i$, which generate environmental damages, $D(E)$, with $D'(E) > 0$, and $D''(E) \geq 0$. The objective of the public firm is to maximise social welfare, defined as

$$W = CS + \Pi + T - D$$

where $\Pi = \sum_{i=0}^{n}$ and $CS = \int_{0}^{Q} (D(t) - p(Q))dt$, or, in the case of a partially privatised public firm, to maximise the following linear combination

$$O = (1 - \theta)\pi_0 + \theta W$$

where $\theta \in [0, 1]$ represents the degree of private ownership in the public firm.

The aforementioned basic framework is developed in several directions, the basic idea being that it is possible to use competition with a public firm as an additional regulatory instrument to improve the performance of an industry but more importantly to address environmental externalities. Hence the defining characteristic here is the interaction of environmental policy with 'regulation by a public firm'. In one of the earliest contributions, Bárcena-Ruiz and Garzón (2006) examine the effects of privatising a public firm in a $n + 1$ oligopoly. In the case of an emission tax, it turns out that privatisation can be detrimental: the effect of the tax makes firms abate their emissions but also leads to a reduction in output, which further exacerbates the underproduction distortion associated with imperfect competition. Having an active public firm remedies this latter distortion by intensifying market competition. Only when the number of private firms is sufficiently large does it make sense to privatise, a result reminiscent of De Fraja and Delbono (1989).[27]

R. Pal and Saha (2014) consider a mixed duopoly under general demand and cost functions and show that the first-best can be implemented while keeping the public firm fully public and using a policy combination of a subsidy on abatement and an output tax. However, given that taxes on output are not common, they also examine the case of a pollution tax, and, as expected, they find that it is not possible to achieve social optimality. In R. Pal and Saha (2015) they further elaborate on the use of a pollution tax but in the context of a differentiated goods duopoly and focus on the issue of optimal privatisation. Because environmental damage is non-monotonic in the degree of privatisation, it is best to have a partially private firm.

---

[27] Wang and Wang (2009) extend Bárcena-Ruiz and Garzón (2006) for the case of differentiated goods but in a duopoly setting and find that environmental damages and social welfare are higher in the mixed duopoly when products are more dissimilar, while Naito and Ogawa (2009) and K. Kato (2011) consider emission standards/quotas and compare to an emission tax. See also Cato (2011), K. Kato (2013), Ohori (2006), and Ohori (2012).

An issue with the papers we have discussed to this point is that firms, whether private or public, decide on their abatement and output choices simultaneously. Lee and Park (2021) remedy this by separating the timing decisions of abatement or 'green R&D' (a long-term decision) and output (a short-term decision). They consider a multi-stage game where the government decides first on regulation instruments (an emission tax or a subsidy to R&D), then in the second stage firms decide on their 'green R&D', and in a final stage they decide on production levels. They also allow for spillover effects in 'green R&D' and examine the question of the relative performance of the two policy instruments in a mixed and private duopoly. The results depend on the efficiency of 'green R&D' and the extent of spillovers. In particular:

> when green R&D is inefficient and the spillover rate is low (high), the government should choose an emissions tax and (not) privatise the state-owned firm. When green R&D is efficient, however, an R&D subsidy is better, but a privatisation policy is not desirable for society, irrespective of spillovers. (Lee & Park, 2021)

Introducing a novel twist, Quarta and Zanaj (2019) provide an interesting analysis where they combine the effects of pollution on health and tie in the role of government as (i) undertaking pollution reducing policies and (ii) participating in healthcare provision by running a public hospital. They do this by using a vertically differentiated model of quality (along the lines of Section 5.1.1) and find that having a public provider improves the average quality of the services provided (and reduces mortality), but surprisingly the mixed duopoly is associated with higher pollution. This latter result is explained by the government having to direct expenditure to both pollution control and provision of health services. Their results point out to the need for a better understanding on modes of public intervention when health and pollution interact.

5.3 Intrinsic Motivation

Up to this point, we have not mentioned issues related to agency and informational asymmetries, and refer the interested reader to the survey by Cavaliere and Scabrosetti (2008). In standard agency theory (exemplified by the principal-agent model), a manager cares about her remuneration (extrinsic reward) but dislikes to expend effort. Hence the principal has to devise an appropriate incentive contract that elicits the required effort from the manager. Private firms are typically more efficient simply because they adopt performance-related pay (PRP) in comparison to public firms operating a fixed remuneration regime. The perceived inefficiency of public firms was one of the main beliefs behind the privatisation waves of the 1980s and beyond; however, when incentive pay is also adopted in a public firm, it turns out that the public firm achieves higher productive efficiency (De Fraja, 1993; Willner & Parker, 2007). Moreover, results of empirical comparisons on efficiency and privatisation are rather contradictory (see, e.g., Megginson and Netter (2001), Florio (2004, 2013), and Mühlenkamp (2015)).

Next we introduce the notion of intrinsic motivation versus extrinsic rewards and explore how their interplay can affect public firm management by shifting the focus from ownership issues (private, public, semi-public) and the objectives of principals (profit or welfare maximisation) towards the selection and motivation of managers in public firms. In this way, we provide a link to behavioural and psychological aspects and discuss some recent contributions that enrich the traditional agency model by incorporating intrinsic motivation and the potential of motivation crowding out (MCO). These issues are pertinent in traditional sectors of public provision and activity, such as health and education.

At its simplest, intrinsic motivation is:

> the doing of an activity for its inherent satisfaction rather than for some separable consequences. (Ryan & Deci, 2000)

Traditional agency theory does not consider intrinsic motivation: the usual performance-related pay (PRP) is an extrinsic reward, while effort only confers disutility to an agent. Taking intrinsic motivation into account, an agent may also derive utility from exerting effort on a task because she adheres to a generalised social norm such as 'honour your contractual obligations' or just wants to engage in the task (*task involvement*). Alternatively, an agent can derive utility due to mission orientation (Besley & Ghatak, 2005) when she cares for the performance of the organisation (*goal identification*).[28] Intrinsic motivation has been recently incorporated into agency theory, notably by Murdock (2002) and James Jr (2005). Following James Jr (2005), and concentrating on the case of task involvement, the utility of an agent can be simply represented as:

$$U = \bar{w} + re - e^2 + I\delta(e - \bar{e}) \tag{12}$$

where $\bar{w}$ is the fixed fee, e stands for effort, r is the incentive pay factor, e^2 is the cost of effort, and I is a binary indicator such that $I = 1$ when the agent is intrinsically motivated and $I = 0$ when she is not. The parameter δ represents

---

[28] See Besley and Ghatak (2018) for an excellent survey on pro-social motivation, Romaniuc (2017) for a historical overview of the concept of intrinsic motivation, tracing it back to Scitovsky (1976) and Frey (1992).

the intensity of intrinsic motivation (Murdock, 2002), while $\bar{e}$ indicates the minimum effort associated with the social norm relating to the task. Thus $\bar{w}+re-e^2$ is the extrinsic motivation of the agent and $I\delta(e - \bar{e})$ the intrinsic motivation. The agent maximises (12) by choosing effort, which yields $\hat{e} = \frac{I\delta+r}{2}$. It is then easy to see that, given $r > 0$, if the agent is already intrinsically motivated in the absence of PRP, she will also do the same when there is PRP, so that there is no motivation crowding out (MCO), as $U(\hat{e}_{I=1}) > U(\hat{e}_{I=0})$. However, there is often concern (as well as extensive evidence from experiments and meta-studies) that intrinsic motivation gets crowded out, repressed by extrinsic rewards or certain forms of control (Weibel et al., 2014). This is especially concerning in the sphere of public entities such as hospitals and schools.

Returning to the issue of productive efficiency and social welfare, Grönblom and Willner (2014) enrich the agency model of James Jr (2005) by (i) considering different organisational forms and (ii) endogenising r and $\bar{w}$.[29] By considering a private monopolist, a public monopoly and a post-privatisation oligopoly, they argue that

> cost differences can go either way, depending on the reward schedule, the public firm's objectives and on social norms or performance targets that affect the presence or absence of intrinsic motivation. Too ambitious social norms or too stringent performance targets may lead to motivation crowding out (MCO), because they make it impossible to derive satisfaction from overperformance. MCO can also lead to fat-cat salaries after privatisation. Changes within an organisation can therefore sometimes have a greater impact than a change of ownership. (Grönblom & Willner, 2014, p. 268)

Undoubtedly, this is an area that needs additional research where, given the non-congruence in organisational objectives in public and private entities, the role of matching principals and agents via appropriate selection rather than incentives becomes paramount. Goal identification may be different in the public sector with employees being more mission-oriented, so an interesting aspect to explore is the adoption of differential motivation schemes in a mixed oligopoly setting. For example, this could be achieved by formulating relevant goal-setting policies in the form of personal standards (Gómez-Miñambres, 2012), or, in the context of mission-oriented entities like not-for-profits, the use of screening contracts with intrinsic motivation determining employees self-selection (Barigozzi & Burani, 2019; Burani, 2021). Finally, in a standard mixed oligopoly setting, De Chiara and Manna (2022) explore the ancillary question of how product market competition may affect firms' decisions to hire altruistic or selfish employees.

---

[29] See also Willner and Grönblom (2020) and Georgellis, Iossa, and Tabvuma (2011).

6 Concluding Remarks

Public firms, despite the extensive privatisation programmes that were implemented since the 1980s, remain an important part of many developed and developing economies. They are present in several strategic sectors in many countries (utilities, energy, infrastructure, transport, minerals, telecommunications, broadcasting, financial services, etc.). Moreover, after the 2008 GFC and the 2019 COVID pandemic, there is an additional interest in public enterprises as suitable vehicles to address several new challenges.

Following the first contribution of Merrill and Schneider (1966) as well as the subsequent seminal papers of De Fraja and Delbono (1989) and Matsumura (1998), the theoretical field of mixed oligopoly has been quite active encompassing a diverse selection of subfields in economics, notably in industrial organisation, applied microeconomic theory, international trade, economics of innovation, to name a few, with the main actor being the public enterprise, linking this field to public economics in general.

The analytical framework of mixed oligopoly, which borrows modelling elements from applied game theory, has proved a resilient and useful tool. The literature on this topic which started with the contribution of Merrill and Schneider (1966) is now extensive. This Element has provided a selective review of the main contributions, while also providing a detailed and step-by-step account of the basic models and the intuition of their results, paying particular attention to discuss the associated market failures.

In recent years, research in this area is moving in new directions by building connections with behavioural and psychological aspects of public firm management. This is not to negate the importance of the traditional analysis of the effects of privatisation and the optimal degree of privatisation that a government should adhere too. In essence, the focus is shifting from traditional public firms (as reviewed in Section 4) to providers of public services (health, education, etc.), environmental issues, and the interface with behavioural traits such as intrinsic motivation of public managers (the main current issues discussed in Section 5). What risked to becoming a démodé topic is now receiving a new impulse with this shift in emphasis. The interaction of private and public entities is simply put a fundamental feature of modern economies.

There are some shortcomings. First, given the vast area of applications and subfields, inevitably there is no general theory of mixed oligopoly. However, this is not something that is unique to this research area. What is clear is that the methodological apparatus of examining a given market where economic actors with differing objectives co-exist has provided some interesting results with distinct policy implications (such as conditions for the desirability or not of privatisation in markets for goods and services characterised by quality considerations; appropriate policy tools for addressing environmental market failures). Second, when considering psychological and behavioural traits, the non-congruence of organisational objectives in public and private entities that brings to centre stage the intricacies of matching principals and agents via appropriate selection rather than incentives becomes paramount. This can be addressed by effectively shifting the traditional focus from ownership consider- ations (private or public) and principals' objectives towards the appropriate and desired motivation of public managers. For sure, we need more research in this area, that is, to explore further the link to behavioural aspects of public provi- sion. Third, the partial equilibrium approach embedded in the traditional mixed oligopoly precludes a priori the examination of several possible objectives of a public enterprise, such as creation of employment, inequality alleviation or other social targets, as well as interaction across markets. This would require a general equilibrium approach, which may be a very ambitious research project.

References

Amir, R., & De Feo, G. (2014). Endogenous timing in a mixed duopoly. *International Journal of Game Theory*, *43*(3), 629–658.

Anderson, S. P., De Palma, A., & Thisse, J.- F. (1997). Privatization and efficiency in a differentiated industry. *European Economic Review*, *41*(9), 1635–1654.

Andolfatto, D. (2021). Assessing the impact of central bank digital currency on private banks. *The Economic Journal*, *131*(634), 525–540.

Andrianova, S., Demetriades, P., & Shortland, A. (2012). Government ownership of banks, institutions and economic growth. *Economica*, *79*(315), 449–469.

Bárcena-Ruiz, J. C., & Garzón, M. B. (2005a). Economic integration and privatisation under diseconomies of scale. *European Journal of Political Economy*, *21*(1), 247–267.

Bárcena-Ruiz, J. C., & Garzón, M. B. (2005b). International trade and strategic privatization. *Review of Development Economics*, *9*(4), 502–513.

Bárcena-Ruiz, J. C., & Garzón, M. B. (2006). Mixed oligopoly and environmental policy. *Spanish Economic Review*, *8*(2), 139–160.

Barigozzi, F., & Burani, N. (2019). Competition for talent when firms' mission matters. *Games and Economic Behavior*, *116*, 128–151.

Barros, F. (1994). Delegation and efficiency in a mixed oligopoly. *Annales d'Economie et de Statistique*, *33*, 51–72.

Barros, F., & Modesto, L. (1999). Portuguese banking sector: a mixed oligopoly? *International Journal of Industrial Organization*, *17*(6), 869–886.

Beato, P., & Mas-Colell, A. (1984). The marginal cost pricing rule as a regulation mechanism in mixed markets. *The Performance of Public Enterprises: Concepts and Measurement* (pp. 81–100), *edited by M. Marchand, P. Pestieau, and H. Tulkens*. Amsterdam: North-Holland.

Benassi, C., Castellani, M., & Mussoni, M. (2016). Price equilibrium and willingness to pay in a vertically differentiated mixed duopoly. *Journal of Economic Behavior & Organization*, *125*, 86–96.

Benassi, C., Chirco, A., & Scrimitore, M. (2014). Optimal manipulation rules in a mixed oligopoly. *Journal of Economics*, *112*(1), 61–84.

Besley, T., & Ghatak, M. (2005). Competition and incentives with motivated agents. *American Economic Review*, *95*(3), 616–636.

Besley, T., & Ghatak, M. (2018). Prosocial motivation and incentives. *Annual Review of Economics*, *10*, 411–438.

Bird, M. G. (2020). State-owned enterprises: Rising, falling and returning? A brief overview. In Luc Bernier, Massimo Florio and Philippe Bance (eds), *The Routledge Handbook of State-Owned Enterprises*, (pp. 60–72). London: Routledge.

Bognetti, G. (2020). History of western state-owned enterprises: From the industrial revolution to the age of globalization. In Luc Bernier, Massimo Florio and Philippe Bance (eds.), *The Routledge handbook of state-owned enterprises* (pp. 25–44). London: Routledge.

Bös, D. (1994). *Pricing and price regulation: An economic theory for public enterprises and public utilities* (Vol. 34). Elsevier.

Bose, A., Pal, D., & Sappington, D. E. (2014). The impact of public ownership in the lending sector. *Canadian Journal of Economics/Revue canadienne d'économique, 47*(4), 1282–1311.

Bris, A. (2023). Credit Suisse: how the mighty fell. *IbyIMD*. Retrieved 2023-06-30, from www.imd.org/ibyimd/finance/credit-suisse-how-the-mighty-fell/.

Brunello, G., & Rocco, L. (2008). Educational standards in private and public schools. *The Economic Journal, 118*(533), 1866–1887.

Burani, N. (2021). No mission? No motivation. On hospitals' organizational form and charity care provision. *Health Economics, 30*(12), 3203–3219.

Cantos-Sánchez, P., & Moner-Colonques, R. (2006). Mixed oligopoly, product differentiation and competition for public transport services. *The Manchester School, 74*(3), 294–313.

Castelnovo, P., & Florio, M. (2020). Mission-oriented public organizations for knowledge creation. In Luc Bernier, Massimo Florio and Philippe Bance (eds.) *The Routledge handbook of state-owned enterprises* (pp. 587–604). London: Routledge.

Cato, S. (2011). Environmental policy in a mixed market: Abatement subsidies and emission taxes. *Environmental Economics and Policy Studies, 13*(4), 283–301.

Cato, S., & Matsumura, T. (2012). Long-run effects of foreign penetration on privatization policies. *Journal of Institutional and Theoretical Economics JITE, 168*(3), 444–454.

Cavaliere, A., & Scabrosetti, S. (2008). Privatization and efficiency: From principals and agents to political economy. *Journal of economic surveys, 22*(4), 685–710.

Ceriani, L., & Florio, M. (2011). Consumer surplus and the reform of network industries: A primer. *Journal of Economics, 102*, 111–122.

Chang, W. W. (2005). Optimal trade and privatization policies in an international duopoly with cost asymmetry. *The Journal of International Trade & Economic Development, 14*(1), 19–42.

Chang, W. W. (2007). Optimal trade, industrial, and privatization policies in a mixed duopoly with strategic managerial incentives. *The Journal of International Trade & Economic Development, 16*(1), 31–52.

Chang, W. W., & Ryu, H. E. (2015). Vertically related markets, foreign competition and optimal privatization policy. *Review of International Economics, 23*(2), 303–319.

Chao, C.- C., & Yu, E. S. (2006). Partial privatization, foreign competition, and optimum tariff. *Review of International Economics, 14*(1), 87–92.

Chiu, J., Davoodalhosseini, M., Jiang, J. H., & Zhu, Y. (2019). *Central bank digital currency and banking* (Tech. Rep.). Bank of Canada Staff Working Paper.

Corneo, G., & Jeanne, O. (1994). Oligopole mixte dans un marche commun. *Annales d'Economie et de Statistique, 33*, 73–90.

Cremer, H., De Rycke, M., & Grimaud, A. (1997). Service quality, competition, and regulatory policies in the postal sector. *Journal of Regulatory Economics, 11*(1), 5–19.

Cremer, H., & Maldonado, D. (2013). Mixed oligopoly in education. CESifo Working Paper, No. 4163, Center for Economic Studies and ifo Institute (CESifo), Munich

Cremer, H., Marchand, M., & Thisse, J.- F. (1989). The public firm as an instrument for regulating an oligopolistic market. *Oxford Economic Papers, 41*(2), 283–301.

Cremer, H., Marchand, M., & Thisse, J.- F. (1991). Mixed oligopoly with differentiated products. *International Journal of Industrial Organization, 9*(1), 43–53.

Dadpay, A., & Heywood, J. S. (2006). Mixed oligopoly in a single international market. *Australian Economic Papers, 45*(4), 269–280.

De Chiara, A., & Manna, E. (2022). Firms' ownership, employees' altruism, and product market competition. *Economic Modelling, 109*, 105774.

De Fraja, G. (1991). Efficiency and privatisation in imperfectly competitive industries. *The Journal of Industrial Economics, 39*(3), 311–321.

De Fraja, G. (1993). Productive efficiency in public and private firms. *Journal of Public Economics, 50*(1), 15–30.

De Fraja, G., & Delbono, F. (1989). Alternative strategies of a public enterprise in oligopoly. *Oxford Economic Papers, 41*(2), 302–311.

De Fraja, G., & Delbono, F. (1990). Game theoretic models of mixed oligopoly. *Journal of Economic Surveys, 4*(1), 1–17.

Delbono, F., & Denicolo, V. (1993). Regulating innovative activity: The role of a public firm. *International Journal of Industrial Organization, 11*(1), 35–48.

Dijkstra, B. R., Mathew, A. J., & Mukherjee, A. (2015). Privatization in the presence of foreign competition and strategic policies. *Journal of Economics, 114*(3), 271–290.

European Commission. (2016). State-owned enterprises in the EU: Lessons learnt and ways forward in a post-crisis context. *European Economy Institutional Paper, 31.*

Eurostat. (2013). *European system of accounts: ESA 2010.* Publications Office of the European Union.

Fershtman, C. (1990). The interdependence between ownership status and market structure: the case of privatization. *Economica, 57*(227), 319–328.

Fjell, K., & Heywood, J. S. (2004). Mixed oligopoly, subsidization and the order of firm's moves: The relevance of privatization. *Economics Letters, 83*(3), 411–416.

Fjell, K., & Pal, D. (1996). A mixed oligopoly in the presence of foreign private firms. *Canadian Journal of economics, 29*(3), 737–743.

Florio, M. (2004). *The great divestiture: Evaluating the welfare impact of the British privatizations, 1979-1997.* MIT press.

Florio, M. (2013). *Network industries and social welfare: The experiment that reshuffled European utilities.* Oxford: Oxford University Press.

Frey, B. S. (1992). Tertium datur: Pricing, regulating and intrinsic motivation. *Kyklos, 45*(2), 161–184.

Fujiwara, K. (2007). Partial privatization in a differentiated mixed oligopoly. *Journal of Economics, 92*(1), 51–65.

Georgellis, Y., Iossa, E., & Tabvuma, V. (2011). Crowding out intrinsic motivation in the public sector. *Journal of Public Administration Research and Theory, 21*(3), 473–493.

Ghandour, Z., & Straume, O. R. (2020). Quality competition in mixed oligopoly. Working paper no. 20, Universidade do Minho. Núcleo de Investigação em Políticas Económicas (NIPE)

Ghosh, A., & Mitra, M. (2010). Comparing Bertrand and Cournot in mixed markets. *Economics Letters, 109*(2), 72–74.

Ghosh, A., & Sen, P. (2012). Privatization in a small open economy with imperfect competition. *Journal of Public Economic Theory, 14*(3), 441–471.

Gil-Moltó, M. J., Poyago-Theotoky, J., Rodrigues-Neto, J. A., & Zikos, V. (2020). Mixed oligopoly, cost-reducing research and development, and privatisation. *European Journal of Operational Research, 283*(3), 1094–1106.

Gil-Moltó, M. J., Poyago-Theotoky, J., & Zikos, V. (2011). R&D subsidies, spillovers, and privatization in mixed markets. *Southern Economic Journal, 78*(1), 233–255.

Godø, H., Nerdrum, L., Rapmund, A., & Nygaard, S. (2003). *Innovations in fuel cells and related hydrogen technology in Norway—OECD case study in the energy sector*. NIFU, skriftserie 35.

Godø, H., & Nygaard, S. (2006). System failure, innovation policy and patents: Fuel cells and related hydrogen technology in Norway 1990–2002. *Energy Policy*, *34*(13), 1697–1708.

Gómez-Miñambres, J. (2012). Motivation through goal setting. *Journal of Economic Psychology*, *33*(6), 1223–1239.

Grilo, I. (1994). Mixed duopoly under vertical differentiation. *Annales d'Economie et de Statistique*, *33*, 91–112.

Grönblom, S., & Willner, J. (2014). Organisational form and individual motivation: public ownership, privatisation and fat cats. *Journal of Economic Policy Reform*, *17*(3), 267–284.

Hamada, K. (2016). Privatization neutrality theorem and discriminatory subsidy policy. Springer Series in Game Theory, in: Pierre von Mouche & Federico Quartieri (ed.), *Equilibrium Theory for Cournot Oligopolies and Related Games: Essays in Honour of Koji Okuguchi* (133–153). Cham: Springer

Hamada, K. (2018). Privatization neutrality theorem: When a public firm pursues general objectives. *The Japanese Economic Review*, *69*, 59–68.

Han, L. (2012). Strategic privatization and trade policies in an international mixed oligopoly. *The Manchester School*, *80*(5), 580–602.

Han, L., & Ogawa, H. (2008). Economic integration and strategic privatization in an international mixed oligopoly. *FinanzArchiv: Public Finance Analysis*, *64*(3), 352–363.

Haraguchi, J., & Matsumura, T. (2016). Cournot–Bertrand comparison in a mixed oligopoly. *Journal of Economics*, *117*(2), 117–136.

Haraguchi, J., & Matsumura, T. (2018). Multiple Long-Run Equilibria in a Free-Entry Mixed Oligopoly. MPRA Paper 86704, University Library of Munich, Germany.

Haraguchi, J., Matsumura, T., & Yoshida, S. (2018). Competitive pressure from neighboring markets and optimal privatization policy. *Japan and The World Economy*, *46*, 1–8.

Harris, R. G., & Wiens, E. G. (1980). Government enterprise: an instrument for the internal regulation of industry. *The Canadian Journal of Economics/Revue canadienne d'Economique*, *13*(1), 125–132.

Hashimzade, N., Khodavaisi, H., & Myles, G. (2007). An irrelevance result with differentiated goods. *Economics Bulletin*, *8*(2), 1–7.

Hehenkamp, B., & Kaarbøe, O. M. (2020). Location choice and quality competition in mixed hospital markets. *Journal of Economic Behavior & Organization*, *177*, 641–660.

Herr, A. (2011). Quality and welfare in a mixed duopoly with regulated prices: the case of a public and a private hospital. *German Economic Review, 12*(4), 422–437.

Heywood, J. S., & Ye, G. (2009a). Delegation in a mixed oligopoly: The case of multiple private firms. *Managerial and Decision Economics, 30*(2), 71–82.

Heywood, J. S., & Ye, G. (2009b). Mixed oligopoly and spatial price discrimination with foreign firms. *Regional Science and Urban Economics, 39*(5), 592–601.

Heywood, J. S., & Ye, G. (2009c). Partial privatization in a mixed duopoly with an R&D rivalry. *Bulletin of Economic Research, 61*(2), 165–178.

Hindriks, J., & Myles, G. D. (2013). *Intermediate public economics*. MIT Press.

Hirose, K., & Matsumura, T. (2019). Comparing welfare and profit in quantity and price competition within Stackelberg mixed duopolies. *Journal of Economics, 126*(1), 75–93.

Ishibashi, I., & Matsumura, T. (2006). R&D competition between public and private sectors. *European Economic Review, 50*(6), 1347–1366.

Ishibashi, K., & Kaneko, T. (2008). Partial privatization in mixed duopoly with price and quality competition. *Journal of Economics, 95*(3), 213–231.

James Jr, H. S. (2005). Why did you do that? An economic examination of the effect of extrinsic compensation on intrinsic motivation and performance. *Journal of Economic Psychology, 26*(4), 549–566.

Jofre-Bonet, M. (2000). Health care: Private and/or public provision. *European Journal of Political Economy, 16*(3), 469–489.

Kato, H. (2008). Privatization and government preference. *Economics Bulletin, 12*(40), 1–7.

Kato, K. (2011). Emission quota versus emission tax in a mixed duopoly. *Environmental Economics and Policy Studies, 13*(1), 43–63.

Kato, K. (2013). Optimal degree of privatization and the environmental problem. *Journal of Economics, 110*(2), 165–180.

Kato, K., & Tomaru, Y. (2007). Mixed oligopoly, privatization, subsidization, and the order of firms' moves: Several types of objectives. *Economics Letters, 96*(2), 287–292.

Klumpp, T., & Su, X. (2019). Price–quality competition in a mixed duopoly. *Journal of Public Economic Theory, 21*(3), 400–432.

Kopel, M., Lamantia, F., & Szidarovszky, F. (2014). Evolutionary competition in a mixed market with socially concerned firms. *Journal of Economic Dynamics and Control, 48*, 394–409.

Kopel, M., & Marini, M. A. (2012). Optimal Compensation Structure in Consumer Cooperatives under Mixed Oligopoly. DIS Technical Reports

2012-06, Department of Computer, Control and Management Engineering, Universita' degli Studi di Roma "La Sapienza".

Kopel, M., & Marini, M. A. (2014). Strategic delegation in consumer cooperatives under mixed oligopoly. *Journal of Economics*, *113*(3), 275–296.

Lahmandi-Ayed, R., Lasram, H., & Laussel, D. (2021). Is partial privatization of universities a solution for higher education? *Journal of Public Economic Theory*, *23*(6), 1174–1198.

Laine, L. T., & Ma, C.- t. A. (2017). Quality and competition between public and private firms. *Journal of Economic Behavior & Organization*, *140*, 336–353.

Lambertini, L. (2013). *Oligopoly, the environment and natural resources*. Routledge.

La Porta, R., Lopez-de Silanes, F., & Shleifer, A. (2002). Government ownership of banks. *The Journal of Finance*, *57*(1), 265–301.

Lee, S.- H., Matsumura, T., & Sato, S. (2018). An analysis of entry-then-privatization model: Welfare and policy implications. *Journal of Economics*, *123*(1), 71–88.

Lee, S.- H., & Park, C.- H. (2021). Environmental regulations in private and mixed duopolies: Taxes on emissions versus green R&D subsidies. *Economic Systems*, *45*(1), 100852.

Levin, R., Klevorick, A., Nelson, R., & Winter, S. (1987). Appropriating the returns from industrial research and development. *Brookings papers on economic activity*, *18*(3, Special Issue on Microeconomics), 783–832. https://EconPapers.repec.org/RePEc:bin:bpeajo:v:18:y:1987:i:1987-3:p:783-832.

Lin, M. H., & Matsumura, T. (2012). Presence of foreign investors in privatized firms and privatization policy. *Journal of Economics*, *107*(1), 71–80.

Lin, M. H., & Matsumura, T. (2018). Optimal privatization and uniform subsidy policies: A note. *Journal of Public Economic Theory*, *20*(3), 416–423.

Lutz, S., & Pezzino, M. (2014). Vertically Differentiated Mixed Oligopoly with Quality-dependent Fixed Costs. *The Manchester School*, *82*(5), 596–619.

Malerba, F. (1993). Italy: The national system of innovation. In R. Nelson (ed.), *National innovation systems: A comparative analysis* (p. 230–259). Oxford: Oxford University Press.

Martimort, D. (2006). An agency perspective on the costs and benefits of privatization. *Journal of Regulatory Economics*, *30*, 5–44.

Matsumura, T. (1998). Partial privatization in mixed duopoly. *Journal of Public Economics*, *70*(3), 473–483.

Matsumura, T. (2003). Endogenous role in mixed markets: A two-production-period model. *Southern Economic Journal*, 403–413.

Matsumura, T., & Kanda, O. (2005). Mixed oligopoly at free entry markets. *Journal of Economics, 84*(1), 27–48.

Matsumura, T., & Matsushima, N. (2003). Mixed duopoly with product differentiation: Sequential choice of location. *Australian Economic Papers, 42*(1), 18–34.

Matsumura, T., & Matsushima, N. (2004). Endogenous cost differentials between public and private enterprises: A mixed duopoly approach. *Economica, 71*(284), 671–688.

Matsumura, T., Matsushima, N., & Ishibashi, I. (2009). Privatization and entries of foreign enterprises in a differentiated industry. *Journal of Economics, 98*(3), 203.

Matsumura, T., & Ogawa, A. (2012). Price versus quantity in a mixed duopoly. *Economics Letters, 116*(2), 174–177.

Matsumura, T., & Okamura, M. (2015). Competition and privatization policies revisited: The payoff interdependence approach. *Journal of Economics, 116*(2), 137–150.

Matsumura, T., & Shimizu, D. (2010). Privatization waves. *The Manchester School, 78*(6), 609–625.

Matsumura, T., & Tomaru, Y. (2012). Market structure and privatization policy under international competition. *The Japanese Economic Review, 63*(2), 244–258.

Matsushima, N., & Matsumura, T. (2003). Mixed oligopoly and spatial agglomeration. *Canadian Journal of Economics/Revue canadienne d'économique, 36*(1), 62–87.

Matsushima, N., & Matsumura, T. (2006). Mixed oligopoly, foreign firms, and location choice. *Regional Science and Urban Economics, 36*(6), 753–772.

Megginson, W. L., & Netter, J. M. (2001). From state to market: A survey of empirical studies on privatization. *Journal of Economic Literature, 39*(2), 321–389.

Merrill, W. C., & Schneider, N. (1966). Government firms in oligopoly industries: a short-run analysis. *The Quarterly Journal of Economics, 80*(3), 400–412.

Moorthy, K. S. (1988). Product and price competition in a duopoly. *Marketing Science, 7*(2), 141–168.

Mühlenkamp, H. (2015). From state to market revisited: A reassessment of the empirical evidence on the efficiency of public (and privately-owned) enterprises. *Annals of Public and Cooperative Economics, 86*(4), 535–557.

Mukherjee, A., & Suetrong, K. (2009). Privatization, strategic foreign direct investment and host-country welfare. *European Economic Review, 53*(7), 775–785.

Murdock, K. (2002). Intrinsic motivation and optimal incentive contracts. *RAND Journal of Economics, 33*(4), 650–671.

Myles, G. (2002). Mixed oligopoly, subsidization and the order of firms' moves: An irrelevance result for the general case. *Economics Bulletin, 12*(1), 1–6.

Nabin, M. H., Nguyen, X., Sgro, P. M., & Chao, C.- C. (2014). Strategic quality competition, mixed oligopoly and privatization. *International Review of Economics & Finance, 34*, 142–150.

Naito, T., & Ogawa, H. (2009). Direct versus indirect environmental regulation in a partially privatized mixed duopoly. *Environmental Economics and Policy Studies, 10*(2–4), 87–100.

Nakamura, Y., & Inoue, T. (2009). Endogenous timing in a mixed duopoly: price competition with managerial delegation. *Managerial and Decision Economics, 30*(5), 325–333.

Nett, L. (1993). Mixed oligopoly with homogeneous goods. *Annals of Public and Cooperative Economics, 64*(3), 367–393.

Nett, L. (1994). Why private firms are more innovative than public firms. *European Journal of Political Economy, 10*(4), 639–653.

OECD. (2017). *The size and sectoral distribution of state-owned enterprises.* OECD.

OECD. (2018). Ownership and governance of state-owned enterprises: A compendium of national practices. OECD.

Oehmke, J. F. (2001). Biotechnology R&D races, industry structure, and public and private sector research orientation. *AgBioForum, 4*(2), 105–114

Ogawa, A., Kato, K. (2006). Price competition in a mixed duopoly. *Economics Bulletin, 12*(4), 1–5.

Ohori, S. (2006). Optimal environmental tax and level of privatization in an international duopoly. *Journal of Regulatory Economics, 29*(2), 225–233.

Ohori, S. (2012). Environmental tax and public ownership in vertically related markets. *Journal of Industry, Competition and Trade, 12*(2), 169–176.

Oliveira, T. (2006). Tuition fees and admission standards: How do public and private universities really compete for students? Discussion Papers in Economics 06/6, Division of Economics, School of Business, University of Leicester.

Pal, D. (1998). Endogenous timing in a mixed oligopoly. *Economics Letters, 61*(2), 181–185.

Pal, D., & White, M. D. (1998). Mixed oligopoly, privatization, and strategic trade policy. *Southern Economic Journal,* 264–281.

Pal, D., & White, M. D. (2003). Intra-industry trade and strategic trade policy in the presence of public firms. *International Economic Journal, 17*(4), 29–41.

Pal, R., & Saha, B. (2014). Mixed duopoly and environment. *Journal of Public Economic Theory*, *16*(1), 96–118.

Pal, R., & Saha, B. (2015). Pollution tax, partial privatization and environment. *Resource and Energy Economics*, *40*, 19–35.

Poyago-Theotoky, J. (1998). R&D competition in a mixed duopoly under uncertainty and easy imitation. *Journal of Comparative Economics*, *26*(3), 415–428.

Poyago-Theotoky, J. (2001). Mixed oligopoly, subsidization and the order of firms' moves: An irrelevance result. *Economics Bulletin*, *12*(3), 1–5.

Quarta, S., & Zanaj, S. (2019). *Health and pollution in a vertically differentiated duopoly* (Tech. Rep.). EERI Research Paper Series.

Romaniuc, R. (2017). Intrinsic motivation in economics: A history. *Journal of Behavioral and Experimental Economics*, *67*, 56–64.

Rostovtzeff, M. I. (1926). *The social & economic history of the Roman Empire*. Clarendon Press.

Ryan, R. M., & Deci, E. L. (2000). Intrinsic and extrinsic motivations: Classic definitions and new directions. *Contemporary Educational Psychology*, *25*(1), 54–67.

Saha, B. (2009). Mixed ownership in a mixed duopoly with differentiated products. *Journal of Economics*, *98*(1), 25–43.

Saha, B., & Sensarma, R. (2011). Mixed ownership, managerial incentives and bank competition. *Bulletin of Economic Research*, *63*(4), 385–403.

Saha, B., & Sensarma, R. (2013). State ownership, credit risk and bank competition: A mixed oligopoly approach. *Macroeconomics and Finance in Emerging Market Economies*, *6*(1), 1–13.

Sanjo, Y. (2009). Quality choice in a health care market: A mixed duopoly approach. *The European Journal of Health Economics*, *10*(2), 207–215.

Sappington, D. E., & Stiglitz, J. E. (1987). Privatization, information and incentives. *Journal of Policy Analysis and Management*, *6*(4), 567–585.

Sato, S., & Matsumura, T. (2019). Shadow cost of public funds and privatization policies. *The North American Journal of Economics and Finance*, *50*, 101026.

Scitovsky, T. (1976). The joyless economy: An inquiry into human satisfaction and consumer dissatisfaction. London: Oxford University Press

Scrimitore, M. (2014). Quantity competition vs. price competition under optimal subsidy in a mixed oligopoly. *Economic Modelling*, *42*, 166–176.

Shapiro, C. (1989). Theories of oligopoly behavior. *Handbook of Industrial Organization*, *1*, 329–414.

Singh, N., & Vives, X. (1984). Price and quantity competition in a differentiated duopoly. *The Rand Journal of Economics*, *15*(4), 546–554.

Stenbacka, R., & Tombak, M. (2020). Competition between for-profit and nonprofit health care providers and quality. *Journal of Institutional and Theoretical Economics, 176*, 243–275.

Stiglitz, J. E., & Rosengard, J. K. (2015). *Economics of the public sector: Fourth international student edition.* WW Norton.

Sutton, J. (1991). *Sunk costs and market structure: Price competition, advertising, and the evolution of concentration.* MIT press.

Tomaru, Y. (2007). Privatization, productive efficiency and social welfare with a foreign competitor. *Research in Economics, 61*(4), 224–232.

Tomaru, Y. (2006). Mixed oligopoly, partial privatization and subsidization. *Economics Bulletin, 12*(5), 1–6.

Tomaru, Y., & Wang, L. F. (2018). Optimal privatization and subsidization policies in a mixed duopoly: Relevance of a cost gap. *Journal of Institutional and Theoretical Economics JITE, 174*(4), 689–706.

Tremblay, C. H., & Tremblay, V. J. (2019). Oligopoly games and the Cournot–Bertrand model: A survey. *Journal of Economic Surveys, 33*(5), 1555–1577.

Van Long, N., & Stähler, F. (2009). Trade policy and mixed enterprises. *Canadian Journal of Economics/Revue canadienne d'économique, 42*(2), 590–614.

Wang, L. F., & Wang, J. (2009). Environmental taxes in a differentiated mixed duopoly. *Economic Systems, 33*(4), 389–396.

Warburton, D. A. (1997). *State and economy in ancient Egypt: fiscal vocabulary of the New Kingdom.* University Press / Vandenhoeck Ruprecht.

Weibel, A., Wiemann, M., & Osterloh, M. (2014). A behavioral economics perspective on the overjustification effect: Crowding-in and crowding-out of intrinsic motivation. *The Oxford Handbook of Work Engagement, Motivation, and Self-Determination Theory*, 72–84.

White, M. D. (1996). Mixed oligopoly, privatization and subsidization. *Economics letters, 53*(2), 189–195.

White, M. D. (2002). Political manipulation of a public firm's objective function. *Journal of Economic Behavior & Organization, 49*(4), 487–499.

Willner, J., & Grönblom, S. (2020). Motivation and performance in state-owned enterprises. In Luc Bernier, Massimo Florio and Philippe Bance (eds.) *The Routledge Handbook of State-Owned Enterprises* (pp. 282–300). London: Routledge.

Willner, J., Grönblom, S., Kainu, A., & Flink, J. (2018). The scope for non-profit objectives in a mixed oligopoly under international competition. *Annals of Public and Cooperative Economics, 89*(2), 415–436.

Willner, J., & Parker, D. (2007). The performance of public and private enterprise under conditions of active and passive ownership and competition and monopoly. *Journal of Economics, 90*, 221–253.

Wu, S.- J., Chang, Y.- M., & Chen, H.- Y. (2016). Imported inputs and privatization in downstream mixed oligopoly with foreign ownership. *Canadian Journal of Economics/Revue canadienne d'économique, 49*(3), 1179–1207.

Zhang, Y., & Zhong, W. (2015). Are public firms always less innovative than private firms? *The Japanese Economic Review, 66*(3), 393–407.

Zikos, V. (2007). Stackelberg mixed oligopoly with asymmetric subsidies. *Economics Bulletin, 12*(13), 1–5.

Zikos, V. (2010). R&D collaboration networks in mixed oligopoly. *Southern Economic Journal, 77*(1), 189–212.

Acknowledgment

I appreciate the guidance received from Massimo Florio (editor) and Chiara Del Bo (associated editor). I also thank the anonymous reviewer whose comments substantially improved this Element. Last but not least, I appreciate the production and editorial support received from Vibhu Prathima Palanisame and Julia Ford and the other members of the Cambridge University Press & Assessment production team. However, any remaining errors and other flaws are my own responsibility.

About the Author

Joanna Poyago-Theotoky is Professor of Economics at the University of Salento, Italy. Her research interests lie in the areas of industrial organization (especially technological innovation, R&D cooperation and research joint ventures), innovation and the environment, and the theory of mixed oligopoly and public firms.

Cambridge Elements $\equiv$

Public Economics

Robin Boadway
Queen's University

Robin Boadway is Emeritus Professor of Economics at Queen's University. His main research interests are in public economics, welfare economics and fiscal federalism.

Frank A. Cowell
The London School of Economics and Political Science

Frank A. Cowell is Professor of Economics at the London School of Economics. His main research interests are in inequality, mobility and the distribution of income and wealth.

Massimo Florio
University of Milan

Massimo Florio is Professor of Public Economics at the University of Milan. His main interests are in cost-benefit analysis, regional policy, privatization, public enterprise, network industries and the socio-economic impact of research infrastructures.

About the Series

The Cambridge Elements of Public Economics provides authoritative and up-to-date reviews of core topics and recent developments in the field. It includes state-of-the-art contributions on all areas in the field. The editors are particularly interested in the new frontiers of quantitative methods in public economics, experimental approaches, behavioral public finance, empirical and theoretical analysis of the quality of government and institutions.

Cambridge Elements ≡

Public Economics

Elements in the Series

A full series listing is available at: www.cambridge.org/PEC

9 781108 726245